D0372480

LIFE IN AND AROUND THE SALT MARSHES

A Handbook of Plant and Animal
Life In and Around the Temperate
Atlantic Coastal Marshes

by MICHAEL J. URSIN
With illustrations by the author

LINDA G. CLARK
Assistant to the author

Thomas Y. Crowell Company   New York   Established 1834

"Tidemarshes: A Vanishing Resource" by George C. Matthiessen originally appeared in *Massachusetts Audubon* in 1962. It is used as an introduction to this book by permission of the author.

Copyright © 1972 by Michael J. Ursin

All rights reserved. Except for use in a review, the reproduction or utilization of this work in any form or by any electronic, mechanical, or other means, now known or hereafter invented, including xerography, photocopying, and recording, and in any information storage and retrieval system is forbidden without the written permission of the publisher. Published simultaneously in Canada by Fitzhenry & Whiteside Limited, Toronto.

Manufactured in the United States of America

L.C. Card 72–78275
Apollo Edition, 1972

To Virginia Ursin, for her outstanding and invaluable assistance in research and editing

Fresh water

Prevailing climate

Visiting
terrestrial life

Food and cover

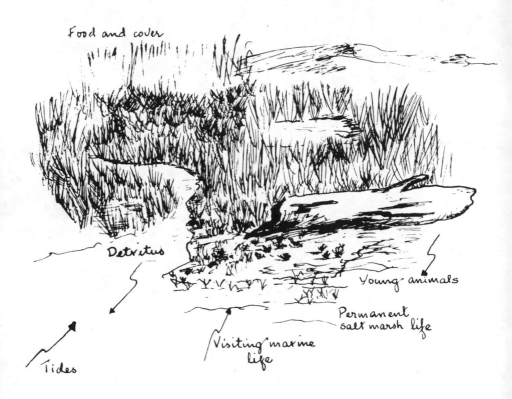

Detritus

Young animals

Permanent
salt marsh life

Visiting marine
life

Tides

PREFACE

The purpose of this book is twofold. First, it is intended to stimulate the layman's interest in the ecologically interesting and important environment of the salt marsh. Second, it is designed to make visits to the salt marshes more interesting, more educational, and more rewarding.

This book is not an encyclopedia, nor is it a complete text. It presents, in as simple a form as possible, descriptions and habitats of plants and animals that are easily and commonly observed. It also includes many species of plants and animals that are frequently encountered in the marshes but are not regular inhabitants.

Taxonomy, or classification, of the plants and animals is utilized at a minimum, and then only to assist those who wish to investigate further. Although it is possible to find different classifications for some species, the system used here is commonly accepted and easily followed.

CONTENTS

INTRODUCTION

TIDEMARSHES: A Vanishing Resource
by George C. Matthiessen, Ph.D.
Marine Research, Inc.

A TIDAL MARSH means different things to different people. To some it is an evil smelling eyesore, a treacherous bog infested with mosquitoes. To others it represents a piece of real estate of great potential value, or an unnecessary obstacle to boating. To many others, hunters and naturalists, it is a haven for a variety of wildlife. And recently, to a growing body of scientists, it represents a dynamic ecosystem of unique biological, geological, and ecological interest and importance.

Tidemarshes are therefore the subject of two basically conflicting points of view: one demands their "improvement"—a polite word for destruction or permanent alteration—while the other urges their preservation. These two opposing concepts are not easily reconciled. Efforts to improve shoreline areas for industrial or recreational purposes, e.g. factory sites, housing developments, navigable channels, and boating facilities, can only increase, not decrease, as coastal population centers expand.

To date this conflict has been one-sided. The people who promise immediate economic benefit are usually more persuasive than the ones who talk in terms of intangible and aesthetic values. Because of the apparent rewards involved, our forebearers were willing to tolerate mass destruction of wildlife, forests, and topsoil. For the same reason we are willing to overlook reckless destruction of our tidal marshes today. We are critical of past generations for the damaged heritage they left us: it would be interesting to know how future generations will feel towards us for dredging and filling tidemarsh areas, altering irrevocably an environment that is as much theirs as ours.

As the nation's population continues to swell, the intangible values of unspoiled shoreline will become less intangible. Seashore vacationers, weekend hunters, and fishermen, will seek unspoiled areas for as long as they exist since macadamized, industrialized shorelines are not what they expect for their recreational investment. In the final analysis, however, it is likely that the greatest economic value of coastal marshes may be found in their effect upon the productivity of adjacent coastal waters.

Many biologists today tend to think of a tidemarsh and the adjacent tidal flats, creeks, and bays surrounding it as a single biological complex, or ecosystem. The water, soil, plants, and animals are woven into a single productive unit, forming the components of a huge, self-renewable, food-producing system. It may be likened to an engine that fuels itself with no help from man and puts out energy, some of which is reconverted into fuel and some of which is converted into food.

How much food does this system produce? It is estimated that tidemarsh ecosystems may produce something in the order of ten tons of organic matter per acre per year.[1] This rate of production compares favorably with terrestrial wheat production under modern and efficient methods of cultivation and is roughly equivalent to intensive sugar cane and rice production. Again, this system operates without benefit of artificial stimulation by man.

Since marsh grass or the algae of marsh creeks is not an important component of our current food supply, it might be asked whether this type of food production is of any conceivable use to man. The answer is that this food is eventually converted into flesh of paramount importance to man, i.e. fish, shellfish, and other edible marine organisms.

In attempting to define how a tidemarsh ecosystem works, biologists often speak in terms of energy. Energy, through metabolic processes, is transferred in many forms through the ecosystem. Some of this energy is "lost" in the form of heat; much is retained within the ecosystem, and it is the amount of energy available that permits the system to produce organic matter in such considerable quantities.

[1] Odum, Eugene P. 1961. *The Role of Tidal Marshes in Estuarine Production.* New York State Conservation Department, "Conservationist," June–July, 1961.

We might say that the initial and fundamental source of energy is derived from the sun through the process of photosynthesis. Radiant energy is incorporated, in the form of organic matter, in the tissues of the marsh grass. The marsh grass, then, serves as a reservoir of potential energy. This energy source is continually being tapped by marsh grass herbivores, bacteria, and mechanical breakdown by waves and tidal flow. In the process, energy in the form of particulate organic matter, or detritus, containing essential nutrients such as phosphates and nitrates, is continually being released into other areas of the ecosystem.

These nutrient salts are as vital to the growth of aquatic plants as they are to that of terrestrial plants. Nitrates and phosphates released from the marsh storehouse are taken up by the microscopic aquatic plants, known as phytoplankton, in the adjacent waters, as well as by the large algae and aquatic spermatophytes, and incorporated into their tissues. They are also taken up by the living marsh grass, to be stored and eventually released. The detritus may be utilized immediately as food by a variety of organisms in the ecosystem, including small fish, shellfish, and crustaceans.

As the phytoplankton flourish on the contributions of the marsh, they form the primary link in the aquatic food chain, a chain that extends through a series of consumers—herbivores and carnivores—and ultimately to a form of food that may be utilized by man, such as the larger fish and shellfish. At all links in this chain, death and decomposition continually occur, making nutrients available in a form that can be used by different plants and animals in the ecosystem.

One of the unique features of the tidemarsh ecosystem is the fact that much nutrient material is not lost but is retained within the system. Tidal mixing and tidal ebb and flow continually distributes nutrient material in its various forms throughout all parts of the system. Because the life cycles of such organisms as bacteria, phytoplankton, and the smaller animals inhabiting the system are relatively short, the turnover is rapid, and nutrients are seldom locked in unusable form for long periods of time. In this way the system is self-sustaining.

Specifically, how do the sea fisheries, and therefore man, benefit from the estuarine-tidemarsh ecosystems along the coastlines? The answer is that many species of tremendous economic value depend upon this type of environment during all or part of their life cycles.

The oyster, for example, thrives in greatest abundance in creeks and estuaries where ocean water is diluted by fresh water draining from the land. Why brackish water areas are highly suitable for this species is due to several factors. However, it may be of particular significance that its diet appears to consist largely of phytoplankton and other particulate organic matter, which as we have seen is linked with the tidemarsh ecosystem.

The shrimp and menhaden provide additional examples of estuarine-dependent animals. The adults of both species are largely oceanic in habitat, and the young are generally spawned at sea. The young, however, seek out the brackish estuaries, which serve as nursery areas during their development. Like the oyster, the shrimp and menhaden subsist largely on the organic material provided in the estuarine-tidemarsh environment.

Even in New England, where tidemarsh areas are less extensive than they are to the south and considerably less extensive than they once were, we have evidence of their role in sustaining the productivity of coastal waters. Why do such highly prized sportsfish as striped bass and bluefish congregate at the mouths of tidal creeks and inlets? How do the bays and estuaries support such large populations of edible shellfish, far greater in terms of weight of protein foods supported per acre than the offshore fishing grounds or, for that matter, terrestrial grazing land for cattle? [2] Why do the young of flounder and menhaden abound in the tidemarsh coves and salt ponds? Again, we can only assume that there is something *special* about these areas, bordered by marshes, that provides sufficient food to attract and sustain these populations.

The natural history of the winter, or blackback flounder is an interesting case in point, particularly as this species represents a commercial fishery of high economic value in Massachusetts and attracts more sportfishermen than any other species. The adult flounder move into the coves and bays during the winter months, and it is here where spawning occurs. The eggs of this species are non-buoyant, adhering in clusters on the bottom until hatching occurs. Because of the negative buoyancy of the eggs and limited motility of the newly-hatched larvae, it is believed that the young tend to remain in the general area in which they were spawned.

During their first year or so the young flounder tend to remain in the relatively shallow water of the estuaries, which are nursery areas for this species as well as for shrimp and menhaden. With increasing age the

[2] Marshall, N. 1960. *Studies of the Niantic River, Connecticut, with Special Reference to the Bay Scallops, Aequipecten irradians.* Limnology and Oceanography, 5:86–105.

flounder move out of the coves and bays in summer. Some may wander considerable distances, eventually to be caught on the offshore fishing grounds. Others may wander relatively short distances, returning to the spawning grounds late in the fall. In the interval they have become available to the sport and commercial fisheries along the coast.

It is believed that the larvae and young of the flounder feed primarily upon the phytoplankton, small worms, mollusks and crustaceans, and marsh detritus. All of these links in the food chain, as we have seen, are bound up in the tidemarsh ecosystem.

It is of interest, then, to consider the history of the commercial fishery for flounder in New England waters. Up until the early 1930's the flounder was the mainstay of the groundfish industry in coastal waters. By the mid-1930's, however, flounder had become so scarce that the dragger fleet was obliged to turn to other species.

What caused this decline? It cannot be attributed solely to increasing levels of pollution in coastal areas, as some of the most heavily polluted bays and estuaries continue to support populations of flounder. Similarly, it is difficult to assign their decline to adverse climatic conditions, as this species is tolerant of a wide range of environmental conditions. It is conceivable that intensive fishing on the spawning grounds, when ripe adults have congregated there in numbers, might be partially responsible, but many such areas were closed to commercial dragging prior to the decline of this species, and many others are too shallow for intensive dragging operations by other than small boats.

It seems highly possible that the decline in flounder abundance may be traced to excessive eagerness to develop the shorelines. Just as birds such as grouse and woodcock require an environment which provides food and cover in order to thrive, so too does the flounder and other species of aquatic organisms. Without the proper environment, they cannot survive.

Since 1914 Connecticut, for example, has lost nearly half of its tidemarsh areas through dredging and filling. If, as we believe, these areas are critical for the flounder as spawning and nursery areas, is it really much wonder that the flounder fishery of southern New England has been significantly affected?

The following statement, contained in the *16th Annual Report of the Atlantic States Marine Fisheries Commission* (1958) reflects the growing concern among marine biologists and fishery administrators about our coastline, and what is happening to it:

"As our knowledge of the biology of our major commercial and sport fishery resources grows, we are becoming more and more impressed with the significance of estuaries and inshore waters, from Maine to Florida, as breeding and nursery grounds for many of the most important species. Whether your chief interest lies in the North, Middle, or South Atlantic region, the condition of the fishery resources is to a large degree dependent upon the condition of these waters.

"Unfortunately, these waters, because they are close to centers of population and industrial development, are particularly vulnerable to effects of human activity; and the rapid growth of population and tremendous industrial expansion of recent years are raising serious problems that may have far more fundamental effects upon the fisheries than any effects produced by fishery activities themselves.

"Perhaps the most serious effects of human activity, though they are not obvious at first glance, are changes produced by alteration of marshlands, for example, drainage and real estate development, deposition of soil from channel dredging, deepening and widening of existing channels, construction of dams and other engineering works, diversion of river runoff for domestic and industrial wastes, which in their most obvious manifestations kill fish and other animals, but which may also have much more subtle and hidden effects upon growth, feeding, spawning and other activities of marine life."

Two points in this statement deserve emphasis. First, the effects that the destruction of the tidemarsh may have upon the ecology of a marine area are extremely subtle in certain respects. Because these effects are not easily measured or readily visible, they may pass unnoticed. This intangible nature of the value of a marsh, of the consequences of its destruction, compounds the difficulty of those who argue for marsh preservation. Perhaps only succeeding generations will fully appreciate these consequences.

The second point is implied in the word "may," which suggests that even the professional biologist cannot state precisely how valuable a specific area of marsh is in terms of its contribution to the fisheries in adjacent waters. Tidemarsh ecology is a very new science that has only recently aroused the interest of biologists. This point underlies the unfortunate

. that we often reach an understanding of the value of a natural resource only after the resource has been damaged beyond repair or is gone completely.

However, ignorance of the exact value of a specific area of marsh should no more justify its misuse than did ignorance justify mismanagement of a few inches of topsoil. It has been estimated that nature required up to 5,000 years to construct some of our Massachusetts marshes. Are we entitled to destroy these marshes in a matter of days simply because no one can tell us its precise economic value? As long as the possibility exists—and recent scientific investigations indicate far more than just a possibility—that there is a relationship between the tidemarsh ecosystem and the productivity of the coastal waters, can we justifiably alter them irrevocably? Our heritage of uncontrollable floods, dust bowls, and extinction of animal species provides the most obvious answer.

EXPLANATORY CHART

In order to simplify the use of this book as a field guide, each section is divided into two parts.

First, there is a brief general discussion of the interrelationships of the plant or animal species. Second, common and important species are presented in chart form for field identification, as shown below.

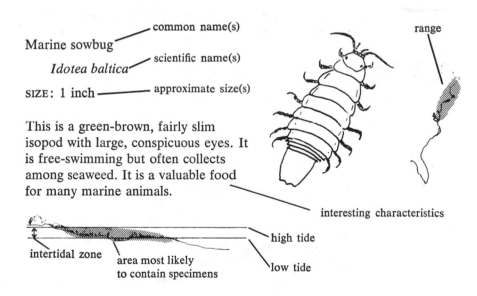

Marine sowbug —— common name(s)

Idotea baltica —— scientific name(s)

SIZE: 1 inch —— approximate size(s)

This is a green-brown, fairly slim isopod with large, conspicuous eyes. It is free-swimming but often collects among seaweed. It is a valuable food for many marine animals.

range

interesting characteristics

high tide

intertidal zone

area most likely to contain specimens

low tide

THE KINDS OF MARSHES

It is impossible to describe life in the marshes as though all marshes were the same. But there are patterns of life that are consistent within all salt marshes. The food chain is the same, and plant life is very similar from marsh to marsh. Species of plants and animals with a high resistance to chemical and temperature changes inhabit nearly all salt marsh areas. For example, the mussel, a common salt marsh dweller, merely closes its shell for lack of water and waits for the tide to return with food and oxygen. Sandworms bury themselves in the sand to stay moist at low tide. Muskrats, seals, turtles, and birds have watertight skins and are protected against such changes.

Life in and around the salt marsh not only is complex but frequently changes. The various features of a salt marsh—tidal creeks, tidal pools, mud flats—all have their own busy environments; their own animal and plant ecosystems; their own problems.

The physical characteristics of the salt marsh influence the quantity and variety of its animal life. A "salt marsh" is a wetland or swamp where the water is basically marine rather than fresh. Unique to salt marshes are the tides. The amount of water in freshwater wetlands can vary due to floods or drought, but this occasional factor has far less effect on the ecology than the predictable tides, which create the important intertidal zone.

The specific landscape of a salt marsh varies with respect to geology and topography. The following diagrams show typical salt marsh designs.

Salt flats (tidal flats) that do not have significant features of terrain, such as pools, creeks, or hills, usually are mud flats which support swimming life twice a day.

Tidal creeks have a salinity the same as or less than that of the ocean. Although their depths vary with the tide, they permanently support swimming species.

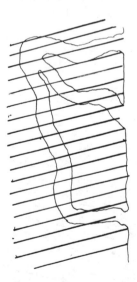

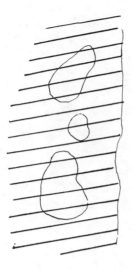

A tidal pool has standing water at all times; only the depth changes with the tide.

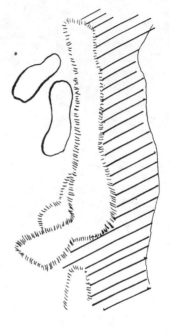

An elevation-protected pool differs in that its depth varies less and is more strongly influenced by rain (reduced salinity) and evaporation (increased salinity).

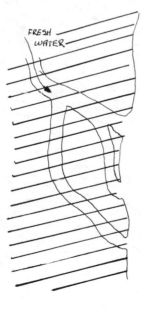

FRESH
WATER

Freshwater streams that empty into the ocean through coastal marshes create brackish-water environments.

MARINE PLANKTON

PHYTOPLANKTON
Phylum CHRYSOPHYTA,
Class *Bacillariophyceae*–Diatoms
Phylum PROTOZOA–Dinoflagellates, etc.

ZOOPLANKTON
Phylum PROTOZOA–Radiolarians, foraminiferans, etc.
Class *Hydrozoa*–Hydroids, medusae
Subclass *Copepoda*–Copepods

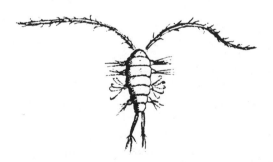

Plankton can be defined as single, one-celled microscopic plants called diatoms, and certain dinoflagellate protozoans, as well as small floating animals that feed on them. These include the larvae of marine species, and animals that live floating in open marine water. Plankton is for the most part dependent on ocean currents for moving about.

Planktonic organisms range in size from smaller than a red blood cell to over a foot in the longest dimension. Most planktonts, particularly planktonic plants, are very small and can be seen clearly only with a magnifying lens.

Plankton can be divided into two distinct groups: phytoplankton, the plant and plantlike species; and zooplankton, the animals. Phytoplankton includes the diatoms (Class *Bacillariophyceae*) and the plantlike organisms called dinoflagellates (Class *Mastigophora*).

The number of species of plankton to be found in the salt marsh is astounding, and their importance to the salt marsh ecology cannot be overstated. They may be considered the "root" of the food chain.

Some of the more common varieties are presented here so that the more resourceful visitor to the salt marsh may have the opportunity to collect and identify a few. Range maps and tidal charts are not used in this section on plankton because, being so widely distributed, its ranges are not easily defined.

PHYTOPLANKTON

DIATOMS—Phylum CHRYSOPHYTA (Class *Bacillariophyceae*)

Diatoms range in size from but a few microns to about one millimeter. Some are able to form chains extending to several centimeters. Many diatoms have elaborate skeletons of silica, called frustules. On the average, diatoms constitute about 90 percent of planktonic material. They are divided into two subclasses: centric diatoms, whose frustules form a pattern that radiates from the center in a somewhat uniform design; and pennate diatoms which are considerably smaller and are cigar-shaped, with a point at each end.

The majority of diatoms collected for study, except those in turbulent, shallow water, will be centric, as the pennate forms are mostly bottom dwellers.

Centric   Pennate

Pleurosigma aestuarii

Biddulphia regia

PROTOZOANS—Phylum PROTOZOA

Dinoflagellates—Order DINOFLAGELLATA

Gymnodinium

This is the organism that creates the "red seas," or "red tide."

ZOOPLANKTON

Zooplankton consists of small floating or weakly swimming animals and the larvae of most marine species. It is divided into two major groups, the protozoans and the metazoans. The protozoans make up a large phylum of one-celled animals, mostly microscopic. There are free-living species that float or swim about, serving as a major food source for many marine animals. The metazoans are many-celled organisms represented by many phyla.

Two major groups of protozoans—foraminiferans and radiolarians—are usually found only in marine waters. Foraminiferans are mostly bottom-dwelling forms, radiolarians mostly floating forms.

Representatives of all the major groups of flagellates, ciliates, and amoebas as well as many sporozoans are found in marine water or living within marine metazoans. The metazoans also include such small multicelled animals as the smaller jellyfishes and the larvae of most marine invertebrates.

PROTOZOANS–Phylum PROTOZOA

Radiolarians

These protozoans are known for their attractive designs. They may be encountered, usually in skeletal form, when searching through the sediments in salt marshes. Their skeletons make up 3 to 4 percent of the ocean floor in the form of "radiolarian ooze."

Hexacontium

Foraminiferans

These are important because of their vast numbers. Most foraminiferans are not planktonic.

This amoeboid protozoan, a planktonic foraminiferan, reproduces in such vast quantities that the minute shells (no larger than a pinhead) make up 65 percent of the ocean's muddy bottom, covering nearly 50 million square miles of the ocean floor.

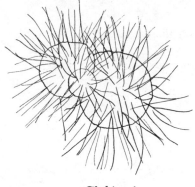

Globigerina

MISCELLANEOUS ZOOPLANKTON

The large variety of zooplanktonts prohibits dealing with each class, subclass, and so on down. The following are a few typical species which may be found on close examination of estuarine water and sediments.

Hydroids, Medusae—Class *Hydrozoa*

Hydrozoans comprise a large class of marine coelenterates (see page 45), some of which go through a complex life cycle. Swimming hydroid larvae settle and develop branches like a plant. The branches bud off tiny medusae jellyfish. The medusae reproduce sexually, producing new hydroid larvae. Medusae differ from true jellyfishes (Class *Scyphomedusae*) in having a membrane, called the velum, across the opening of the bell.

Euphausids

Euphausids are important ocean planktonts. They are found in the northern seas in such numbers that they are a primary food for the great filter-feeding whales.

Amphipods, Isopods

Amphipods and isopods, such as the familiar sandhopper, are dealt with at large under the section on animal life, but very small species and young forms can be considered planktonic. Their habitat is varied, and they may be abundant in tidal pools.

Copepods—Subclass *Copepoda*

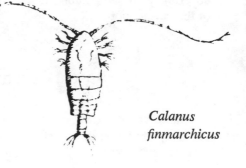

Subclass *Copepoda* (meaning "oar-footed") is the most abundant animal group in the world! Copepods are small segmented invertebrates with double-branched swimming feet. They play an important role in the marine world as the food link between diatoms and the larger animals of the ocean.

Calanus finmarchicus

Crustacean Plankton

There are several larval forms of crustaceans. Many of these smaller forms are inhabitants of tidal pools, tidal creeks, and other parts of the intertidal zone. Crustaceans have as many as six preadult stages: nauplius, cypris, protozoea, zoea, mysis, megalops. In some species some of the stages occur in the egg; in other species these stages are free-swimming or floating and are important members of the planktonic community.

Cypris larva of a barnacle

Balanus sp.

Nauplius larva of a barnacle

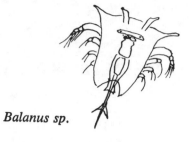

Balanus sp.

Zoea larva of a crab

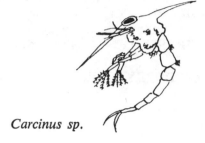

Carcinus sp.

Megalopa larva of a crab

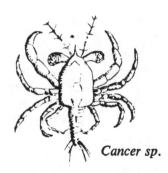

Cancer sp.

Fish Eggs

As the salt marsh is an important spawning ground for many fish, eggs are often found in tidal pools and elsewhere in the intertidal zone, both free-floating and in sediments. They can easily be confused with a variety of other planktonts.

Atlantic mackerel egg

Scomber scombrus

PLANT LIFE IN THE SALT MARSH

MARINE ALGAE (SEAWEEDS)

Phylum CYANOPHYTA (MYXOPHYCOPHYTA)—Blue-green algae
Phylum CHLOROPHYTA—Green algae
Phylum PHAEOPHYTA—Brown algae
Phylum CHRYSOPHYTA—Yellow-green algae, yellow-brown algae, and
    diatoms
Phylum RHODOPHYTA—Red algae

SALT MARSH GRASSES, SEDGES, AND RUSHES AND MISCELLANEOUS HIGHER PLANTS

Family *Gramineae*—Grasses
Family *Polygonaceae*—Buckwheats
Family *Juncaceae*—Rushes
Family *Chenopodiaceae*—Goosefoots, spinaches
Family *Caryophyllaceae*—Pinks
Family *Primulaceae*—Primroses
Family *Compositae*—Composites
Family *Amaranthaceae*—Amaranths
Family *Rosaceae*—Roses
Family *Orchidaceae*—Orchises
Family *Scrophulariaceae*—Figworts
Family *Potamogetonaceae (Zosteraceae)*—Pondweeds
Family *Plantaginaceae*—Plantains
Family *Typhaceae*—Cattails
Family *Cyperaceae*—Sedges
Family *Plumbaginaceae*—Leadworts
Family *Iridaceae*—Irises

An overall look at a marsh reveals different zones of life, indicated by different colors. Depending upon the type of marsh, there will be wider and narrower zones. This zonation is not restricted to plant life but includes the native animals as well. It is easy to see the plants that restrict themselves to one zone or another; it is less obvious, but just as important, that certain animal species do the same.

The inland portion of the salt marsh—the driest area—supports plants unable to withstand frequent flooding. Salt meadow cordgrass (*Spartina patens*) grows abundantly in this upper zone. Where the tide floods the plants, the taller salt marsh cordgrass (*Spartina alterniflora*) is predominant. As you proceed toward the ocean, you will find a belt of eelgrass (*Zostera marina*), which prefers deep and frequent immersion.

Another interesting zone, and an active one, is where a sandy beach or dune meets the tidal flat or marsh, creating an ecotone—an area where two distinctly different environments are intermixed. A great variety of life is usually found here as it is a changing environment, similar to the shore of a pond or the edge of a forest.

In this section, algae (seaweeds) are dealt with first. Rooted algae appear in distinct zones. The upper intertidal zone supports blue-green algae; the intermediate intertidal zone has primarily brown algae; and at the low-tide mark, where it is wet most of the time, red algae are predominant. Plankton in the form of small floating algae is present in large quantities throughout the marsh. The surf and tides also bring in algae which may not be indigenous.

The herbaceous plants (those that do not form woody stems) are presented next. Most of them range throughout the temperate Atlantic coast. Predominantly grasses, these plants are a highly productive group and an important part of the ecosystem. While alive, they serve as food for many animals and as cover for young mammals, birds, and fish. When they die, the resulting detritus is a key food in ocean ecology.

Not every species of plant life is included here. Instead, to help orient the visitor to various areas of the salt marsh, the common and easy-to-locate varieties are selected.

MARINE ALGAE

Algae can be thought of as simple plants that live in water, both fresh and marine. Marine algae are generally referred to as seaweeds, except for the microscopic, one-celled forms of **Phylum CHRYSOPHYTA,** Class *Bacillariophyceae*—the diatoms (see page 6).

Through the years, seaweeds have been grouped by color because those closely related botanically are usually the same color. For example, the seaweeds of **Phylum RHODOPHYTA** are mostly some shade of red. The size of marine algae ranges from the microscopic diatoms to the giant kelps, which can be several hundred feet long.

The smaller algae are an important food for many marine animals. The larger varieties, such as rockweeds and kelps, are not commonly eaten, but after they die and are attacked by bacteria, they form a detritus food staple for thousands of marine species in all oceans.

Most seaweeds need a hard surface, which they attach to by means of a holdfast. Some are free-floating; a few fucoids **(Phylum PHAEOPHYTA)** change in the marshes to a dwarf variant without holdfasts.

Many seaweeds, which are not native to the marshes, are found on tidal flats and in pools and creeks, having broken loose from their holdfasts and been brought in by the tide or a stormy surf. Some of these are included here because they are so frequently found in the marsh.

Classification of marine algae is extensive and complicated, and beyond the scope of this book. Thus only five phyla are presented with little further classification; and several species of each, likely to be encountered by a visitor to the marshes, are described.

BLUE-GREEN ALGAE—Phylum CYANOPHYTA

The blue-green algae are an inconspicuous phylum represented by some 1,500 species, marine and freshwater. Most of these appear as scum on mud and rocks or form a fuzzy surface on larger plants and floating objects. They are microscopic plants of simple construction and reproduce by simple division.

Callothrix sp.

SIZE: Filamentous plants up to ⅒ inch

Above the high-tide mark *Callothrix* forms a band of blackish-brown feltlike substance that crumbles (powders) to the touch, on rocks, driftwood, and other plants. When wet it has a slimy feel.

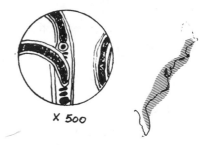

X 500

Rivularia atra

SIZE: Filamentous plants, appearing in colonies a few inches across

Colonies appear as irregular blackish-green wet masses. They are commonly found on tidal creek banks and under dead salt marsh grasses.

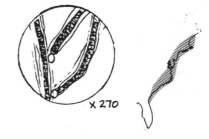

X 270

Mermaid's-hair

Lyngbya majuscula

SIZE: Microscopic individual plants, forming threads up to 1 yard long

This is an important alga for soil formation or stabilization. It forms a compact surface on soft mud, providing a roothold for other plants. In pools, filaments break off and form a blackish-green or purple threadlike scum, often filled with gas bubbles, on the surface.

GREEN ALGAE—Phylum CHLOROPHYTA

Green algae include more than 5,000 species, most of which live in fresh water or damp soil. Marine species are more common in tropical waters. Green algae reproduce both by cell division, as do blue-green algae, and by forming sex cells (gametes).

Ulothrix flacca

SIZE: Forms whiskerlike strands of up to 1 inch, in colonies that cover rocks, pilings, and similar surfaces

This alga thrives throughout the intertidal zone. It grows rapidly, forming a hairy green mat on hard, stationary surfaces. It is predominant in the spring.

Prasinocladus lubricus

SIZE: Tiny branching filamentous plants

This is a northern alga that forms a thin coating on pebbles and salt marsh grasses in tidal pools.

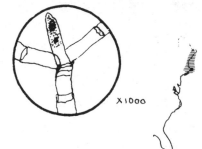

X1000

Enteromorpha intestinalis

SIZE: Fronds up to 1 foot long, ½ inch wide

This seaweed is aptly named, as the green fronds or branches resemble intestines. It grows in shallow water and tidal pools.

16

Enteromorpha erecta

SIZE: Fronds 4 to 8 inches long

Enteromorpha erecta attaches to hard surfaces, such as shells, in exposed areas. The plants are soft to the touch.

Enteromorpha linza

SIZE: Up to 15 inches high

Enteromorpha linza can be confused with sea lettuce (*Ulva lactuca*) as they both have flat yellow-green fronds, but close examination will show tubular stems on this alga.

Sea lettuce

Ulva lactuca

SIZE: Up to 2 feet high

The yellow-green frond of this alga closely resembles lettuce. It grows between the tidal limits. Pieces frequently break loose and can be found along the beach and floating in tidal pools.

Monostroma oxyspermum

SIZE: 1 to 4 inches; up to 2 feet in protected pools

This alga is partial to shallow water and favors brackish conditions. It is commonly found in salt marsh creeks where there is a freshwater outflow. *Monostroma oxyspermum* is easily confused with *U. lactuca*.

Chaetomorpha melagonium

SIZE: Filamentous plants up to 1 foot long

Most species of *Chaetomorpha*, including *C. melagonium,* differ from other green algae in that the individual cells can be seen with the naked eye. Furthermore the filaments do not branch, as is true of *Cladophora.*

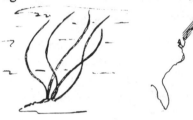

Cladophora gracilis

SIZE: Filamentous plants 1 foot or more long

Instead of the characteristic bright green of *Chaetomorpha* and *Rhizoclonium*, this seaweed appears more gray-green. A close look will reveal distinct branching.

Rhizoclonium sp.

SIZE: Filamentous plants up to several inches long

This is a genus of small filamentous algae with a few branches. It is common on mud and sand flats and in brackish waters. *Rhizoclonium riparum* forms yellowish mats on mud flats and rocks in the intertidal zone.

Codium fragile

SIZE: Up to 3 feet

Codium fragile appeared only recently on our shores, apparently an import from Europe. It is easily distinguished by its large cylindrical dark green branches, usually forming a "Y".

BROWN ALGAE—Phylum PHAEOPHYTA

Most brown algae are wholly marine and prefer cold water. The rockweeds (*Fucus*) and the kelps (*Laminaria, Agarum,* and *Alaria*) are the conspicuous members of this group.

Rockweed, fucus

Fucus vesiculosus

SIZE: 1 to 3 feet

The most common brown alga within our range, this predominates in the upper intertidal region. It is easily recognized by the small paired air bladders and flat branches. At the tips of the branches are the reproductive sacs.

Rockweed, marsh fucoid

Fucus vesiculosus var. spiralis

SIZE: 10 to 12 inches high

In salt marshes, *F. vesiculosus* exists in a distinctly smaller form known as *var. spiralis*. The branches are twisted, with very few air bladders. Its reproductive cycle is simplified and lacks the characteristic holdfasts. This salt marsh variety is known as a marsh fucoid. In the upper regions of the marsh, where the freshwater influence is greatest, *var. spiralis* has fewer air bladders or visible reproductive sacs. Other variants of *F. vesiculosus,* such as *var. sphaerocarpus* and *var. laterifructus,* differ somewhat from *var. spiralis* but are also small, simplified plants adapted to upper intertidal life.

Rockweed

Fucus spiralis

SIZE: Up to 12 inches long

This is another rockweed in our area that is without air bladders. It grows in bushy clumps with regular branching. It usually grows higher in the intertidal zone than *F. vesiculosus* and *Ascophyllum nodosum.*

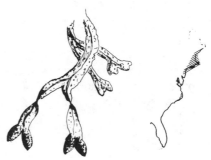

Wrack, bladder wrack

Ascophyllum nodosum

SIZE: 1 to 2 feet long

This is a very common rockweed that inhabits the middle-to-lower intertidal region. It can easily be distinguished from the *Fucus* rockweeds by examining the branches. *Ascophyllum* has a round-to-oval branch, as opposed to the flat branch of *Fucus*. It attaches itself to rocks by means of disklike holdfasts. Large clumps of this seaweed when stranded by low tide retain a great deal of moisture, serving as shelter for many marine organisms.

Sargassum

Sargassum filipendula

SIZE: 1 to 2 feet long

This alga does not originate in the Sargasso Sea, as the name would seem to imply, but rather is the commonest offshore brown seaweed in the warmer part of our range. It is usually found washed ashore by the surf.

Kelp, sugar kelp

Laminaria saccharina

SIZE: Stalk, 4 to 5 inches; blade, 6 feet or longer

The "leaves" (blades) of this large kelp are often found on beaches and tidal flats in colder regions.

Kelp

Laminaria agardhii

SIZE: 6 feet or longer

When one speaks of "kelp" on the central United States Atlantic coast, chances are he is referring to this seaweed, as it is the most common kelp in our area. It is distinguished from its northern cousin *L. saccharina* by narrower blades. The salt marsh visitor will see only loose blades of this alga that have broken away from its usual habitat below the low-tide line.

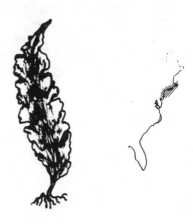

Kelp

Alaria esculenta

SIZE: Up to 10 feet long and 6 inches wide

This is a northern kelp, occasionally found south of Cape Cod. It grows in exposed areas from the low-tide mark seaward. The edge of the blade tears easily, giving it a ragged appearance.

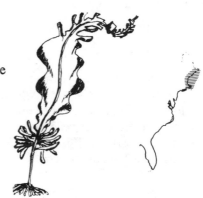

22

Kelp

Agarum cribrosum

SIZE: Up to 5 feet long

The perforated blade makes this alga easily recognized. It is a northern kelp, preferring colder waters, and grows just below the low-tide mark.

YELLOW-GREEN, GOLDEN-BROWN ALGAE; DIATOMS—Phylum CHRYSOPHYTA

This phylum includes three major classes of algae: *Xanthophyceae,* the yellow-green algae, which are—with the exception of *Vaucheria sp.*—important only as freshwater algae; *Chrysophyceae,* the golden-brown algae, which are unlikely to be recognized by the average visitor to the salt marsh; and *Bacillariophyceae,* the diatoms (see page 6).

Vaucheria sp.

SIZE: Microscopic

Vaucheria is mentioned here because of its importance as a soil former in the salt marshes. Its tiny filaments form a mat on salt flats, creating a suitable base for other plants to root.

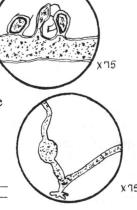

X 75

X 75

RED ALGAE—Phylum RHODOPHYTA

Red algae appear red-to-purplish-black because of a red pigment, r-phycoerythrin, which masks the characteristic green of chlorophyll. The more than 2,500 recognized species of these algae prefer deeper water. Some species are of economic value for the production of agar-agar, for food, and for chemicals.

Irish moss

Chondrus crispus

SIZE: 2 to 6 inches

Irish moss is a food in northern Europe as well as a source of chemicals for industry. It forms dense purplish-green masses in tidal pools, creeks, and other standing water in the marshes. It prefers the cooler regions and grows actively throughout the year.

Dulse

Rhodymenia palmata

SIZE: Up to 15 inches

North of Cape Cod, *R. palmata* is occasionally collected for food. It is a dark wine-red and grows in somewhat deeper water than *Chondrus* or *Gigartina*.

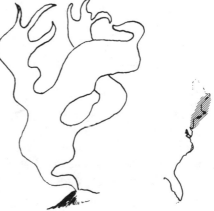

Gigartina stellata

SIZE: Up to 2 feet

Closely related to *C. crispus, G. stellata* prefers the lower tidal pools and exposed rocky shores in even colder regions. It is most active in the winter.

Bangia fuscopurpurea

SIZE: 4 to 8 inches

The dark red-purple color and unbranched filaments (examined with a hand lens) will distinguish *B. fuscopurpurea* from other algae in the upper intertidal zone.

Rhodochorton purpureum

SIZE: Forms colonies ½ by ½ inch

Rhodochorton purpureum appears as tiny red mounds growing on rocks in the intertidal zone. It is made up of minute branching filaments, discernible only with a magnifying glass.

Porphyra umbilicalis

SIZE: 4 to 12 inches long

This is another alga collected for food. It resembles sea lettuce except for its purple-to-brown color.

Nemalion multifidum

SIZE: 9 inches high

This is a summer alga which forms a slimy surface on rocks. It is irregularly branched; occasional specimens are found without branching.

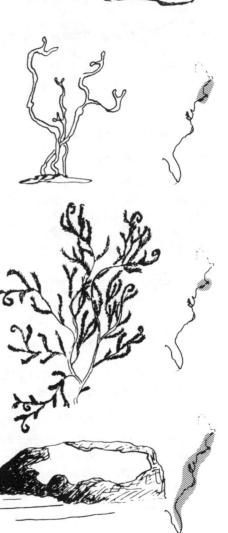

Asparagopsis hamifera

SIZE: 4 inches high

This is not a salt marsh alga, but the bright red asparaguslike plants are frequently broken loose and found on tidal flats. The curled ends of some of the branches help to identify it.

Hildenbrandia prototypus

SIZE: Microscopic individual plants

This is one of the commonest red algae on the Atlantic coast. It forms an orange-red-to-brownish-red crusty surface (becoming purple with age) on rocks and shells.

Agardhiella tenera

SIZE: 8 inches high

This alga is very hard to distinguish from several other red seaweeds. Of varied color, it attaches to rocks and shells and has a coarse, bushy appearance.

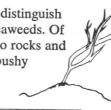

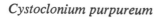

Cystoclonium purpureum

SIZE: Up to 24 inches

This is another very common bushy red alga. It varies in color from purple-red to brown. Washed-up plants are abundant in the early summer.

Ceramium rubrum

SIZE: 5 inches high

There are several species of *Ceramium* in our area, *C. rubrum* being the most common. Although it grows from the low-tide mark out, it is easily collected in the tidal wash. Color can vary from red to brown to green. It will attach to nearly any substrate or may remain free-floating. This alga can be identified by the banded branches and tiny, clawlike branch tips.

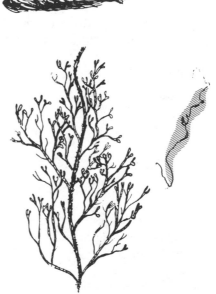

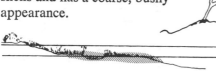

Ahnfeltia plicata

SIZE: 2 to 8 inches high; stalks 1/16 inch in diameter

Ahnfeltia plicata forms stiff, wiry, bushy tufts. The plant is multibranched and dark red—almost black. The narrow stalks are hard to the touch.

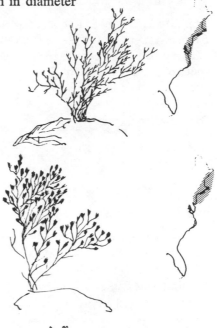

Polysiphonia lanosa

SIZE: 2 inches

This is an interesting alga in that it grows only on *Ascophyllum nodosum* (see page 21). It forms small, stiff, nearly black tufts which do not collapse when removed from the water.

Seirospora griffithsiana

SIZE: Filamentous plants 2 to 6 inches long

This is an alga that grows on other seaweeds, eelgrass, shells, and stones. The lateral branches alternate and end in clustered tips.

enlarged

Callithamnion corymbosum

SIZE: 2 inches

If you find small, delicate, spherical masses of pink algae—almost like cobwebs—on eelgrass or various seaweeds, they are probably *C. corymbosum.*

enlarged

SALT MARSH GRASSES, SEDGES, AND RUSHES AND MISCELLANEOUS HIGHER PLANTS

GRASSES—Family *Gramineae*

Salt meadow grass, salt hay, marsh grass

Spartina patens

SIZE: 6 to 33 inches

Spartina patens characteristically falls over when it ages, forming a mat through which the next year's growth emerges.

Smooth cordgrass, salt marsh cordgrass

Spartina alterniflora

SIZE: 4 inches to 7 feet

This grass can stand wetter conditions than *S. patens* and ranges into the intertidal zone. It provides cover for both marine and terrestrial animals.

Salt reed grass

Spartina cynosuroides

SIZE: 3 to 9 feet
Perennial

This is a tall grass with a preference for brackish water. The spikes are brown-to-purple.

Freshwater cordgrass

Spartina pectinata

SIZE: 2 to 6 feet
Perennial

Spartina pectinata prefers brackish
water and is likely to be found where
freshwater streams empty into the salt
marsh.

Spike grass, alkali grass

Distichlis spicata

SIZE: 4 inches to 3½ feet
Perennial

Spike grass grows in clumps around the
edges of tidal pools, along tidal creeks,
and at the high-tide mark—usually
where there are considerable salt
deposits.

Reed

Phragmites communis

SIZE: 4 to 13 feet
Perennial

This reed commonly grows along
ditches in a hedgelike manner.

Black grass

Juncus gerardi

SIZE: 6 to 32 inches
ACTIVITY: June–September

The seed capsule of black grass has
vertical purple stripes. This species
tolerates a great deal of salt and is
found in a variety of marine
environments.

GOOSEFOOTS—Family *Chenopodiaceae*

Seabeach orach

Atriplex arenaria

SIZE: 2 feet
ACTIVITY: July–October
Annual

The leaves are gray-green, the stem
tinged with red. It has small greenish
flowers.

Typical orach

Atriplex patula

SIZE: Up to 5 feet
ACTIVITY: July–October
Annual

Atriplex patula can be identified by
the distinctly triangular leaves, tiny
green flowers, and arrowhead-shaped
seeds.

Woody glasswort, leadgrass, perennial saltwort

Salicornia virginica

SIZE: 1½ to 2½ inches
ACTIVITY: August–October
Perennial

This glasswort has asparaguslike tips.
They are green in the summer,
turning gray in the fall.

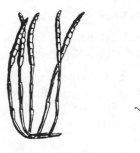

Woody glasswort

Salicornia bigelovii

SIZE: ½ to 4 inches
ACTIVITY: August–November
Annual

Salicornia bigelovii is found in "salt
pans," around pools where the salt
concentration is high, and at the
high-tide line. It turns red in the fall.

Chicken claws, pigeon foot, samphire

Salicornia europaea

SIZE: ½ to 4 inches—occasionally to 15 inches
ACTIVITY: August–November
Annual

In the fall *S. europaea* turns yellow,
then orange, then red. It has distinct
branches—as opposed to *S. virginica*,
which grows in unbranched stalks.

Sea blite

Suaeda maritima

SIZE: 2 to 16 inches
ACTIVITY: July–October

The stem of this plant is tinged with red. The pale green flowers—from one to four of them—grow out of the axis of leaf and stem.

Coast blite

Chenopodium rubrum

SIZE: Up to 32 inches
ACTIVITY: August–November
Annual

The coast blite has small light red flowers, growing in clusters and becoming scarlet in the autumn. The main branches radiate outward at the roots.

PINKS—Family *Caryophyllaceae*

Sand spurry

Spergularia marina

SIZE: Up to 14 inches
ACTIVITY: June–October
Annual

Sand spurry has thick, fleshy leaves. In late summer it shows pink flowers.

PRIMROSES—Family *Primulaceae*

Sea milkwort

Glaux maritima

SIZE: 1 to 13 inches
ACTIVITY: June–July
Perennial

Sea milkwort will grow in most soils
that are saline or brackish. It has
bell-shaped flowers that may be white,
purple, or pink.

COMPOSITES—Family *Compositae*

Seaside goldenrod

Solidago sempervirens

SIZE: 8 inches to 7 feet
ACTIVITY: July–November

Thick leaves and brilliant golden-yellow
flowers in the fall make this attractive
salt marsh plant easy to identify.

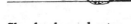

Slender-leaved aster

Aster tenuifolius

SIZE: 6 to 24 inches
ACTIVITY: August–October
Perennial

This aster has an attractive purple
flower in the fall. The single or forked
stems have thin, flexible leaves.

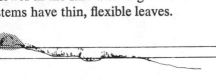

Marsh elder, highwater shrub

Iva frutescens var. oraria

SIZE: Up to 10 feet
ACTIVITY: August–October
Perennial

This is a larger flowering shrub
growing at the outer edge of the marsh
and high up on the beaches. Its flower
is greenish-white.

Groundsel tree, sea myrtle, consumption weed

Baccharis halimifolia

SIZE: 3 to 9 feet
ACTIVITY: August–October
Perennial

This treelike shrub has large, coarsely
toothed leaves and grows from the
outer edge of the marsh to well inland.

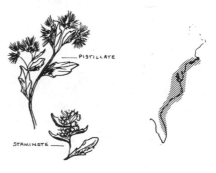

Salt marsh fleabane, stinkweed

Pluchea purpurascens var. succulenta

SIZE: Up to 4½ feet
ACTIVITY: August–September
Annual

This is a fairly large plant with thick
stems and toothed leaves. In the fall it
has clusters of pink-to-purple flowers.

37

AMARANTHS—Family *Amaranthaceae*

Seabeach amaranth

Amaranthus pumilus

SIZE: Blades ½ to 1 inch
ACTIVITY: July–October
Annual

The leaves are crowded at the ends of
the branches; the stems are very fleshy.
It is found frequently on Nantucket and
Martha's Vineyard and is occasionally
encountered south to North Carolina.

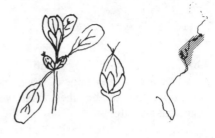

ROSES—Family *Rosaceae*

Silverweed

Potentilla anserina

SIZE: 1 to 3 feet
ACTIVITY: June–August

The undersides of the leaves have a
silvery appearance, giving the plant
its name. It grows on runners and has
bright yellow flowers in the summer.

ORCHISES—Family *Orchidaceae*

Common ladies' tresses, screw auger

Spiranthes cernua

SIZE: 4 to 24 inches
ACTIVITY: August–September
Perennial

This is a marsh orchid with spiraling
stalks of yellowish-white flowers.

FIGWORTS—Family *Scrophulariaceae*

Seaside gerardia

   Gerardia maritima

SIZE: 2 to 12 inches
ACTIVITY: July–September
Annual

This is a small, single-stemmed
(occasionally branched) figwort with
pink-to-purple flowers. The leaves
may have a purple tinge.

PONDWEEDS—Family *Potamogetonaceae*

Eelgrass

   Zostera marina

SIZE: Up to 3 feet

Not a true grass at all, *Z. marina* is
the most common plant growing in the
shallows beyond the low-tide mark.

PLANTAINS—Family *Plantaginaceae*

Early seaside plantain

   Plantago juncoides var. decipiens

SIZE: 2 to 8 inches
ACTIVITY: June–August
Perennial

The early plantain has narrow leaves
and small off-white flowers.

Late seaside plantain

Plantago oliganthos

SIZE: 2 to 8 inches
ACTIVITY: July–September
Perennial

Late plantain has thick leaves that
are triangular in cross section.

CATTAILS–Family *Typhaceae*

Cattail

Typha latifolia

SIZE: 3 to 8 feet
ACTIVITY: May–July
Perennial

Cattails are probably the best
indicators of fresh water in the salt
marsh, as they grow in both brackish
marsh and freshwater environments.
Typha latifolia has gray-green leaves.

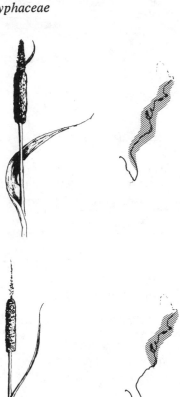

Cattail, narrow-leaved cattail

Typha angustifolia

SIZE: 2 to 5½ feet
ACTIVITY: May–July
Perennial

A smaller plant than *T. latifolia*, it
also has narrower leaves and smaller
"tails."

SEDGES—Family *Cyperaceae*

Sedge

Cyperus polystachyos var. texensis

SIZE: 4 to 8 inches
ACTIVITY: July–October

This is a fairly thick-stemmed plant with yellow-to-brown spikes at the ends of the branches. It grows in damp sand or soil.

Salt marsh bulrush

Scirpus maritimus

SIZE: 1 to 3 feet
ACTIVITY: July–October
Perennial

The stems of *S. maritimus* are green, the spikelets brown. The stems are distinctly three-sided. It is most populous above the high-tide mark.

Chairmaker's rush

Scirpus americanus

SIZE: 1 inch to 5 feet
ACTIVITY: June–September
Perennial

The dark brown stem of this rush is stout and hard. It prefers brackish waters and even grows in freshwater marshes.

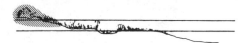

Horned rush

Rhynchospora macrostachya

SIZE: 6 inches to 3 feet
ACTIVITY: July–October
Perennial

The horned rush prefers a sandy or
peat soil. It has ten to thirty
red-brown spikelets.

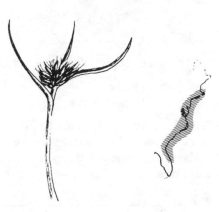

LEADWORTS—Family *Plumbaginaceae*

Sea lavender, marsh rosemary

Limonium carolinianum

SIZE: 6 to 24 inches
ACTIVITY: July–October

The base of the stems of *Limonium*
are thick and woodlike. In the early
fall it has light purple flowers.

IRISES—Family *Iridaceae*

Blue-eyed grass

Sisyrinchium arenicola

SIZE: 6 to 21 inches
ACTIVITY: May–July
Perennial

The flowers easily identify this plant.
They are blue-to-violet with a little
yellow star in the center.

MARINE INVERTEBRATES—THE LOWER ANIMALS

Phylum PROTOZOA—Plankton
Phylum PORIFERA (POROZOA)—Sponges
Phylum COELENTERATA (CNIDARIA)—Coelenterates (hydroids, true jellyfishes, sea anemones, corals)
Phylum CTENOPHORAE—Comb jellies
Phylum PLATYHELMINTHES—Flatworms
Phylum NEMERTINA (NEMERTEA)—Ribbonworms
Phylum CHAETOGNATHA—Arrowworms
Phylum PHORONIDA—Phoronid worms
Phylum BRYOZOA—Moss animals
Phylum BRACHIOPODA—Lampshells
Phylum SIPUNCULIDA (SIPUNCULOIDEA)—Peanut worms
Phylum ECHIUROIDEA—Echiuroid worms
Phylum ECHINODERMATA—Echinoderms (sea urchins, starfishes)
Phylum CHORDATA—Invertebrate chordates
Phylum ANNELIDA—Segmented worms, lugworms
Phylum ARTHROPODA—Arthropods (crabs, shrimp, etc.)
Phylum MOLLUSCA—Mollusks (snails, bivalves, squid, chitons)

To be an invertebrate, an animal must lack a backbone. It can be just about any shape and size. There are nearly a million known species of invertebrates, and there will likely be many more when scientists have named and classified them all.

These animals comprise approximately twenty-eight phyla. So varied and complex are they that changes in their taxonomy are frequent, and there is not complete agreement on existing nomenclature.

This section deals with twelve phyla, representing the marine invertebrates that are ecologically important to the salt marsh. The average observer will never see most of the invertebrate species. However, some, such as the soft-shell ("steamer") clam *(Mya arenaria),* are familiar to nearly everyone.

Invertebrates are a distinct link in the food chain. Detritus nourishes them, and they are in turn a principal food for vertebrates as well as for many of the larger invertebrates themselves.

The ranges and habitats of invertebrates are largely dependent on the nature of the species. Rock barnacles, for example, are restricted to rocky shores and relatively stationary hard surfaces. Jellyfish, on the other hand, may be found in tidal pools or well out to sea, as they are somewhat dependent on tides, currents, and weather conditions.

As with salt marsh plants, the large number of invertebrates prohibits dealing with every species. In this book, the common and important ones (with the exception of insects, which are not included) are discussed.

SPONGES—Phylum PORIFERA

Tufted sponge

Scypha lingua

SIZE: Up to 1 inch long

This sponge may be found among seaweeds, shells, and stones close to the low-water mark. It is yellowish-white and may have buds.

Red sponge

Microciona prolifera

SIZE: Forms masses up to 1 foot high and 6 inches across

The red sponge develops in irregular masses and appears bright red. It grows on shells, rocks, or nearly any hard object.

Dead man's fingers

Haliclona oculata

SIZE: 3 to 6 inches long

At low tide these sponges appear as little pale orange plants. Their bleached skeletons are often found on the shore.

COELENTERATES—Phylum COELENTERATA

Snail fur

Hydractinia echinata

SIZE: "Hairs" 1/16 inch long

Snail fur appears as a growth of hair on snail shells inhabited by hermit crabs, and on rocks, seaweeds, deadwood, and the like. It is very common and is often taken for an alga or fungus. The organism is orange-to-cream in color—sometimes brown.

Double-branching hydroid, cup hydroid

Obelia dichotoma

SIZE: Forms colonies up to 1 inch high

This hydroid lives in treelike pink colonies on eelgrass in the intertidal zone.

Many-rayed jellyfish

Aequorea forskalea

SIZE: 4 to 6 inches across bell

This jellyfish is often found in estuaries and harbors. It varies in color from dark brown to red, blue, or yellow. Fifty or more radial canals are distinct. It is most common in the autumn.

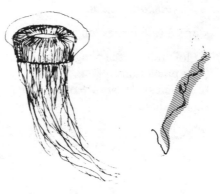

Silvery hydroid

Thuiaria argentea

SIZE: Forms colonies up to 1 foot across

This hydroid appears in bushy, silvery branches. The medusae are planktonic. Branches often break off and can be found free-floating.

Tidal creek bordered by *Spartina sp*.

The salt marsh at Parker River Wildlife Refuge, Newburyport, Mass.
The red plant is *Salicornia bigelovii*.

Above: A tidal pool.

Left: A tidal creek
at low tide.

Above right: Green crab
(Carcinus maenas).

Right: Blue, or soft-shell,
crab *(Callinectes sapidus)*.

Lady, or calico, crab *(Ovalipes ocellatus).*

Blue crab, or soft-shell crab *(Callinectes sapidus)*, with eggs.

Painted turtle *(Chrysemys picta).*

Above left: Rock crab *(Cancer irroratus).*

Left: Spider crab *(Libinia emarginata).*

Blackback, or winter flounder *(Pseudopleuronectes americanus)*.

Eggs of the common tern *(Sterna hirundo)*.

Double-crested cormorant *(Phalacrocorax auritus)*. (John E. Swedberg)

Herring gulls *(Larus argentatus)*. (John E. Swedberg)

Osprey *(Pandion halieatus).* (Scott-Swedberg)

Above: Osprey with flounder. (Scott-Swedberg)

Left: Juvenile mute swan *(Cygnus olor).* (John E. Swedberg)

Adult mute swan (John E. Swedberg)

White-tailed, or Virginia, deer *(Odocoileus virginianus)*. (Scott-Swedberg)

Sun jellyfish

Cyanea capillata

SIZE: Up to 3 feet across bell—occasionally larger; tentacles, 75 to 200 feet long

Jellyfishes are not regular residents of the salt marsh, but as they are partial to bays and coastal areas, they may be found in tidal pools. *Cyanea capillata* is a large jellyfish that prefers the cooler coastal waters. It is brown-to-purplish-red. Its tentacles have stingers.

Moon jellyfish

Aurellia aurita

SIZE: 6 to 10 feet across

This is a very common jellyfish. It is bluish-white with yellow or pink markings in a four-leaf clover arrangement. Its numerous tentacles have small stingers.

Pallid sea anemone

Diadumene leucolena

SIZE: Up to 1 inch

This translucent white, pink, or green anemone has a long, cylindrical body and attaches to oysters and rocks.

Worm sea anemone

Ceriantheopsis americanus

SIZE: Up to 6 inches extended

This species can be distinguished from other anemones by its two rows of tentacles and lack of cross bands. It can be found in sandy, muddy, and rocky areas at the low-tide mark. It is brown in color.

Star coral

Astrangia danae

SIZE: Forms colonies up to 4 inches across

This is the only coral in this area. It is mentioned because the attractive white skeletons are found almost anywhere. The live animal lives in clear shallow water, is pink or white, and captures its prey with stinging cells.

COMB JELLIES—Phylum CTENOPHORAE

Pear comb jelly

Mnemiopsis leidyi

SIZE: Up to 6 inches

This is a pear-shaped jellyfish that may be very abundant in shallow water. If disturbed, the fine hairs on its body luminesce blue-green.

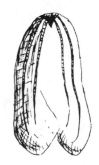

Sea walnut, sea gooseberry

Pleurobrachia pileus

SIZE: Body, ¾ inch; tentacles, up to 15 inches

This species may be pink, yellow, or clear, with two branched tentacles for catching plankton. It is more abundant in the winter and inhabits the shallows as well as the deep ocean.

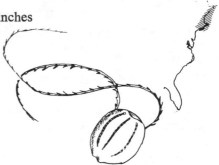

Slipper comb jelly

Beroe cucumis

SIZE: Up to 4 inches

This comb jelly eats plankton as well as other jellyfish. It is an open-water invertebrate but may be found in tidal pools, having been left there at high tide.

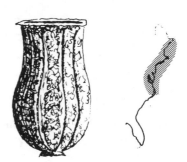

RIBBONWORMS—   **Phylum NEMERTEA**

Pink sandworm

Cerebratulus lacteus

SIZE: Up to (but rarely) 6 feet long, 1 inch wide

This is a pink or cream-colored worm with brown bands.

ARROWWORMS—Phylum CHAETOGNATHA

Arrowworm

Sagitta hexaptera

SIZE: Up to 2½ inches

The arrowworm inhabits the open ocean but occasionally will appear in coastal waters in great numbers. It is a translucent grayish-brown.

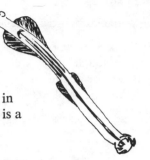

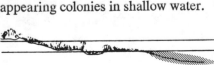

MOSS ANIMALS—Phylum BRYOZOA

Common moss animal

Crisia eburnea

SIZE: Forms colonies ½ to ¾ inch high

Although an individual moss animal is but ⅟₆₄ inch high, its ability to colonize makes it easy to locate. It "roots" firmly on the bottom at the low-tide mark and on seaweed, and subsists on detritus and plankton.

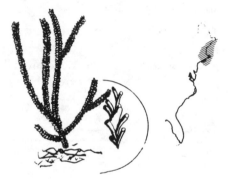

Fringed moss animal

Crisia denticulata

SIZE: Forms colonies up to 1 inch high

This moss animal grows in fluffy-appearing colonies in shallow water.

Turreted moss animal

Bugula turrita

SIZE: Forms colonies up to 12 inches high

The large colonies of this moss animal
are cream-colored and have yellow
or orange tentacles. The colony is
shaped very much like a miniature tree.

Sea mat

Membranipora monostachys

SIZE: Microscopic, forming visible colonies

Sea mat forms an irregular coating on
hard surfaces, such as shells and rocks,
and on some drying seaweeds—usually
Laminaria or *Fucus*. It is commonly
seen dead, as a crust. When alive it is
yellow or cream-white, flexible, and
shows small spines. It can easily be
mistaken for an alga.

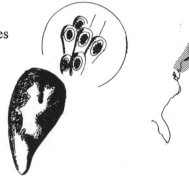

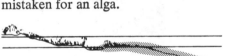

LAMPSHELLS—Phylum BRACHIOPODA

Horny lampshell

Glottidia pyramidata

SIZE: 1 inch long

As the tide recedes, the lampshell
moves into its sand burrow to stay wet.
It is white-to-greenish-white with
green markings.

Green brittle star

Ophioderma brevispinum

SIZE: Center disk ½ inch

The color of the brittle star varies from greenish-brown to nearly clear green, sometimes with bands. This starfish may be found in tidal pools, on sand flats, or well out to sea.

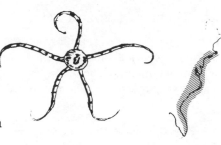

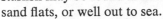

Purple sea urchin

Arbacia punctulata

SIZE: Test, 2 inches wide; spines, 1 inch long

Among the seaweed in tidal pools the purple sea urchin lives on a variety of organic matter in the water. Except for the bare dome, the test is covered with purplish-brown spines and has red feet.

Green sea urchin

Strongylocentrotus droehbachiensis

SIZE: Test, 3½ inches wide; spines, ½ inch long

Although this sea urchin is found as far south as New Jersey, it inhabits salt marsh ponds only as far south as Cape Cod. Bright green spines completely cover the test.

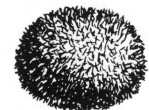

Pallid sea cucumber

Cucumaria pulcherrima

SIZE: 1½ to 2 inches long

This yellow-to-white cucumber-shaped animal, with ten branched tentacles at one end, is found among eelgrass in muddy shallows.

Wormlike sea cucumber

Leptosynapta inhaerens

SIZE: 8 inches long, ⅜ inch in diameter

This is a slender, nearly white sea cucumber with twelve branched tentacles. Soft and translucent, it can be found on either sandy or muddy bottoms.

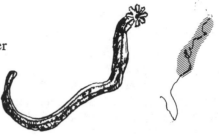

SEGMENTED WORMS—Phylum ANNELIDA

Sea mouse

Aphrodite hastata

SIZE: 7 inches long, 2 inches wide

This worm does not look like a worm. Rather it is more like what its name implies—a legless mouse—with green iridescent hairs on its sides.

Smooth-scaled worm

Harmothoe imbricata

SIZE: 2 inches long

This worm is usually found among mussels. It has thirty-seven segments and is brown.

Smaller clam worm

Nereis succinea

SIZE: Up to 5 inches

The clam worm is a good swimmer and fast burrower. Inexperienced fishermen have been pinched by the sharp jaws of these creatures when using them for bait. The smaller clam worm is nocturnal, predatory, and brownish.

Plumed worm

Diopatra cuprea

SIZE: 12 inches

The plumed worm is an odd-looking creature found on the tidal flats. It has a shiny blue-green body, tentacles in front, and bright red bushy gills on its anterior third. These worms are often seen in groups partially buried in shallow water.

Coiled worm

Spirorbis borealis

SIZE: ⅛ inch long

This little worm lives in a spirally coiled shell with nine branched green gills visible at its anterior opening. It is found among seaweeds.

ARTHROPODS—Phylum ARTHROPODA

Horseshoe crab

Limulus polyphemus

SIZE: Up to more than 2 feet long

Except to those totally unfamiliar with the seashore, the horseshoe crab is a well-known member of the coastal community. In the spring when it spawns, it comes in large numbers into the shallows—particularly where there are clams, one of its favorite foods.

Northern goose barnacle

Lepas fascicularis

SIZE: Shell 2 inches

This is the only barnacle in our area that attaches by a stalk. It grows in colonies on floating objects. Its shell is white and thin.

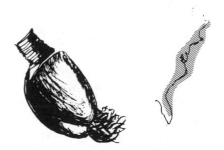

Rock barnacle

Balanus balanoides

SIZE: Up to ⅜ inch wide

Between the tide lines, *B. balanoides* attaches to rocks and other stationary objects. It is white, smooth, and lives on organic material floating in the water, which it filters out with its cirri.

Marine sowbug

Idotea baltica

SIZE: 1 inch

This is a green-brown, fairly slim isopod with large, conspicuous eyes. It is free-swimming but often collects among seaweed. It is a valuable food for many marine animals.

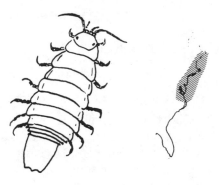

Gribble

Limnoria lignorum

SIZE: ¼ inch long

This tiny animal is mentioned here because it is representative of a valuable food source for shore birds and fish. To locate it, flip over a piece of driftwood near the low-tide mark, as a bird would; you will probably see small holes bored by gribbles, and likely a specimen or two.

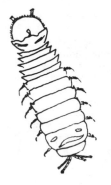

Long-horned sand flea

Talorchestia longicornis

SIZE: 1 inch long

This small amphipod is mainly active at night—when most shore birds are not. It jumps about erratically and burrows out of sight rapidly in moist sand. It is white and has long antennae.

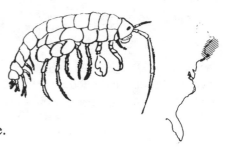

Common sand flea

Orchestia platensis

SIZE: ½ inch

This sand flea is brown with rust-colored antennae. Disturb a clump of damp seaweed, and likely a number of them will hop about, as though avoiding a feeding bird.

Seaweed hopper

Gammarus locusta

SIZE: Up to 1 inch

Under seaweed, stones, or driftwood *G. locusta* lies on its side, and scurries off at the first sign of danger. It is an excellent swimmer and can be found in deep water. It is brown with yellow-orange markings.

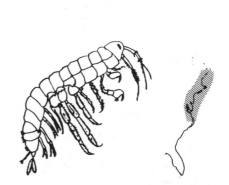

Skeleton shrimp

Aeginella longicornia

SIZE: 1 inch

At the low-tide mark this small, slender shrimp moves about the eelgrass in strange bending motions. Its green-brown color makes it difficult to detect.

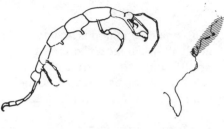

Edible shrimp

Penaeus aztecus

SIZE: Up to 6 inches

Though not a true salt marsh resident, this brown-green shrimp prefers shallow waters and may easily be found in tidal creeks or trapped in tidal pools. It makes excellent eating and is commercially harvested.

Sand shrimp

Crangon septemspinosa

SIZE: 2 inches

The sand shrimp can be found almost anywhere there is standing water. Its greenish, translucent body makes it difficult to see.

Common grass shrimp

Palaemonetes vulgaris

SIZE: 1 inch

This small, translucent shrimp is common in tidal pools and creeks. You can distinguish it by the reddish-brown spots on its shell.

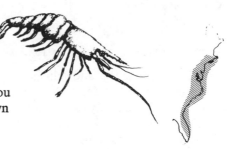

Mantis shrimp

Squilla empusa

SIZE: Up to 1 foot long

In spite of its size, the mantis shrimp is not seen frequently, as it burrows in the mud. It is yellow-green, with a red tail.

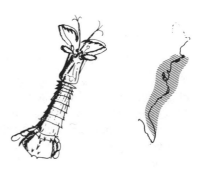

Hermit crab

Pagurus pollicaris

SIZE: 5 inches

Hermit crabs are unique because of their habit of living in empty snail shells. The crab is red-brown.

Common spider crab

Libinia emarginata

SIZE: Carapace up to 4 inches long

Its extremely long legs and spiny carapace make the spider crab easy to identify. It is commonly found in oyster beds among rocks, and on the muddy bottoms of bays and estuaries. Although it is naturally brown-to-tan, algae frequently grow on it, changing its appearance.

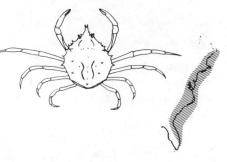

Green crab

Carcinus maenas

SIZE: Carapace up to 2½ inches long

The green crab is a pugnacious character common in shallow water over a rocky bottom. At night it can be found at the shoreline with a flashlight. It is a strong green, with yellow markings.

Marsh fiddler crab

Uca pugnax

SIZE: Carapace 1 inch wide

This is probably the best-known small crab in the tidal marshes. The one outsized claw on the male identifies him. The color is usually steel-blue, but sometimes it shows other colors.

China-back fiddler crab

Uca pugilator

SIZE: Carapace 1¼ inches wide

In the southern part of our range, this fiddler crab forages about in the drier parts of the marsh.

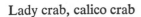

Lady crab, calico crab

Ovalipes ocellatus

SIZE: Carapace up to 2½ inches wide

Swimming crabs differ from "walking" crabs in that the last pair of legs is flattened to a paddle shape. *Ovalipes ocellatus,* an excellent swimmer, also can bury itself in wet sand with astounding speed.

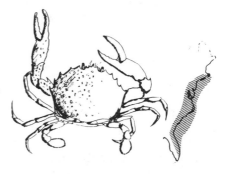

Blue crab, soft-shell crab

Callinectes sapidus

SIZE: Carapace up to 7 inches wide

"Soft-shell" refers to a blue crab that has just shed, leaving it with a new, soft shell. This crab is prized for its meat and is a widely sought-after seafood. The blue crab depends on the salt marshes for its early life. It is the only species with a sharp spike extending from each side.

Rock crab, red rock crab

Cancer irroratus

SIZE: Carapace up to 5 inches wide

The rock crab is common along the Atlantic coast. When the tide is in, it forages among plants and rocks in the intertidal zone. It is red-brown—often yellow-brown—with red markings.

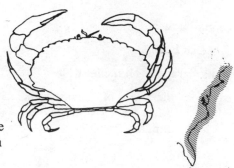

Flat mud crab

Eurypanopeus depressus

SIZE: Carapace 1 inch wide

This is a small crab, gray-brown with black claw tips. It is an aggressive animal and readily nips at intruders. Its legs have more hair than do most other crabs.

Oyster crab

Pinnotheres ostreum

SIZE: Carapace ¾ inch

Where you find oysters, you will likely find this small crab. It is white with a pink tinge. Its carapace is nearly round.

Little keyhole limpet

Diodora cayenensis

SIZE: Up to 2 inches long

As the name implies, the opening in the top of the shell is keyhole-shaped. It ranges in color from white to gray; the inside shell is white-to-bluish-gray.

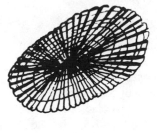

Tortoise-shell limpet

Acmaea testudinalis

SIZE: 1½ inches long

The exterior of the oval shell ranges from light blue-gray to white; inside it is dark brown with a white border around the opening, flecked with brown near the top. It is frequently found in tidal pools.

Little chink shell

Lacuna vincta

SIZE: Up to ⅜ inch long

This is a pretty little snail, white to light brown, sometimes with purple bands. Its shell, with its characteristic small chink on the side, is often found on tidal flats after a storm.

Common periwinkle

Littorina littorea

SIZE: Up to 1 inch long

The common periwinkle is abundant throughout the lower intertidal zone. Although most specimens are an olive-brown, they may vary considerably, from black to tan. There is a white band around the shell opening. These periwinkles make delicious and easily prepared eating, though they are often overlooked as a food.

Smooth periwinkle

Littorina obtusata

SIZE: Up to ½ inch

The smooth periwinkle prefers the wetter regions of the intertidal zone, attaching to rocks and rockweed (*Fucus sp.*). It is yellow-brown, frequently with a brown spiral.

Rough periwinkle

Littorina saxatilis

SIZE: Up to ½ inch

The rough periwinkle is commonly found in the driest regions of the intertidal zone. It is gray, with yellow-to-brown bands.

Salt marsh periwinkle

Littorina irrorata

SIZE: 1 inch

The various periwinkles usually restrict themselves to a particular zone. *Littorina irrorata* is found on wet vegetation between the tide marks. It is an off-white, with lines of brown dots following the spiral.

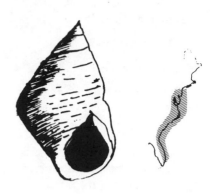

Common boat shell

Crepidula fornicata

SIZE: Up to 2 inches

The boat shell is one of the most common mollusks found on the tidal flats and in tidal pools after the tide recedes. Many of the shells are an attractive dark purple inside. The outside is off-white, often flecked with brown.

STACK OF BOAT SHELLS

Shark eye

Polinices duplicatus

SIZE: Up to 2½ inches long

The shell is medium brown with a suggestion of blue. It is generally a little wider than high, giving it a flattened appearance.

PINKISH-BROWN
OPERCULUM
"DEAD SAILORS TOE NAILS"

Common moon shell

Lunatia heros

SIZE: 4 inches

The common moon shell is white-to-brown outside. It burrows in the sand and attacks mollusks.

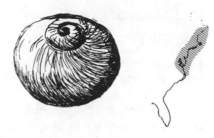

Oyster drill

Urosalpinx cinerea

SIZE: Up to 1 inch

This is an attractive snail to look at but a serious nuisance in oyster beds, where it preys on oysters by actually drilling holes in their shells. It is gray-to-yellow, with a purple-to-brown opening.

Rock purple

Thais lapillus

SIZE: Up to 2 inches

Although the name implies that this snail is purple, it is usually white or yellow. A gland in the animal, when properly prepared, once produced the "royal purple" of kings' robes, from which it earned its name.

Mottled dog whelk

Nassarius vibex

SIZE: ½ inch

This is a small, thick-shelled snail; the shell is white-to-light-brown, with beaded ridges. Like *Thais lapillus,* it preys on bivalves.

New England dog whelk

Nassarius trivittatus

SIZE: Up to ¾ inch long

This whelk, one of the more attractive snails, is light yellow, sometimes with a few brown bands. Beaded lines, evenly spaced, run from top to bottom around the shell.

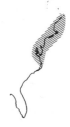

Mud snail

Nassarius obsoletus

SIZE: Up to 1 inch

The mud snail is active, leaving a trail in the mud or sand. It appears black at a distance, but actually the color varies from dark brown to dark blue.

Blue mussel

Mytilus edulis

SIZE: Up to 3 inches

This is a much neglected seafood, although one of the tastiest. The shell has no ribs, is blue-black with light patches, and often shows growth marks, like rings on a tree stump. It is found in clusters on rocks.

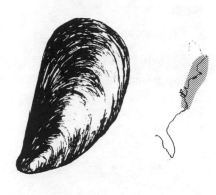

Ribbed mussel

Modiolus demissus

SIZE: 3 to 4 inches long

Edible, but not as tasty as other mussels and clams, the ribbed mussel is easily identified by the sharp ridges running the length of the shell. Its color varies from shades of red to brown to green.

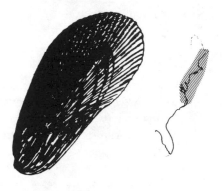

Atlantic nut clam

Nucula proxima

SIZE: ¼ inch

This tiny clam is often mistakenly called a baby soft shell (*Mya arenaria*). Its valves are commonly found at the shoreline with slipper shells, mussel shells, and the like. It is a translucent white.

Bay scallop

Aequipecten irradians

SIZE: Up to 3 inches

Few seashores are not covered with the shells of this mollusk. Its color varies greatly. It is tasty, and easily available because of its preference for shallow water. The bay scallop is unique among mollusks in that it is an excellent swimmer and has a set of eyes.

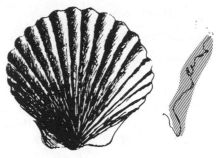

Carolina marsh clam

Polymesoda caroliniana

SIZE: 1 inch

This is an oval clam that resides in the southern marshes.

Northern quahog

Mercenaria mercenaria

SIZE: Up to 5 inches

This is a heavy-shelled clam, usually white, and is especially appetizing when eaten raw or in chowder. The Indians used its shell to make wampum for currency and decorative beads.

Virginia oyster

Crassostrea virginica

SIZE: Up to 6 inches

On the half shell at the table or attached to a rock in an estuary, this bivalve is as well known as any. Its popularity and economic value exceed even those of the steamer clam. It has an irregular surface, gray with white markings, and a rough edge. It grows in clusters on rocks or large shells in bays and brackish ponds.

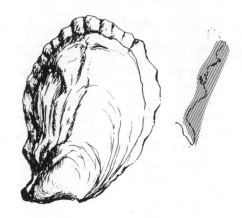

Baltic macoma

Macoma balthica

SIZE: Up to 1½ inches

This is a medium-sized clam, white and often with a pink-to-red tinge. It is common on the intertidal flats and is often confused with small quahogs.

Stout razor

Tagelus plebeius

SIZE: Up to 4 inches

This is a yellow-to-white rectangular clam that is found in intertidal mud.

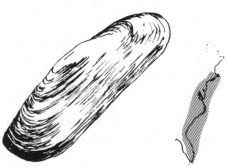

Common soft-shell clam, steamer clam

Mya arenaria

SIZE: 1 to 6 inches (average 3½ inches)

This is the clam of clam chowder, steamed clams, fried clams, and baked clams. It varies in color, depending upon the sand it grows in, from white (in white sand) to nearly black (in black sand).

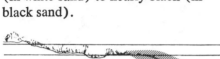

Common basket clam

Corbula contracta

SIZE: ½ inch

This is a small white clam, fatter than the soft-shell variety. It has concentric rings on its shell.

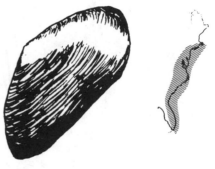

False angel wing

Petricola pholadiformis

SIZE: Up to 2½ inches

When digging for steamers (*Mya arenaria*) you may come across an irregularly shaped white shell with ridges. This is the false angel, which is also found burrowed in gravel.

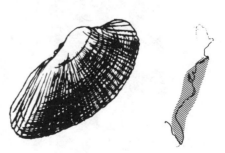

MARINE VERTEBRATES—THE HIGHER ANIMALS

Class *Aves*—Birds
Class *Reptilia*—Turtles, snakes
Class *Mammalia*—Mammals
Class *Chondrichthys*—Sharks, skates, rays
Class *Osteichthys*—Bony fish

Vertebrate life in the marshes is made up of birds, fish, reptiles, and mammals. Of these, the birds are the most frequently seen; the least seen are the mammals. Fish are present in large schools at high tide or in the tidal pools and creeks at low tide. Most of them are young ocean species that, when grown and able to fend for themselves, head for the open ocean, returning to the salt marshes only to spawn.

The average visitor to the salt marsh will see a large variety of birds, their species varying with the season. He may catch a glimpse of a water snake, or a deer grazing in the salt meadow hay at a distance. The schools of fish he may see will be hard to identify without netting them for close examination; and even then, without a fair knowledge of icthyology, it will be difficult to distinguish many species.

There is no overstating the importance of vertebrate life in the salt marsh, particularly fish and birds. Their roles in the marsh are indispensable to the ecology. The marsh is intrinsic to their livelihoods: to fish for spawning, for protection of the young, and for food production for many species; to birds for nesting, feeding, and hiding in the vegetation; to reptiles and mammals searching for food. In the summer the marsh appears particularly active with vertebrate life. In the winter, too, it is active, though not so obviously. Blackback flounder breed in the winter, the fry depending on the winter marsh for the first phase of their lives. Many shore birds, such as the eider, winter in the Atlantic marshes, returning to their summer nesting grounds in the Arctic with the first sign of spring.

In the pages that follow, a number of common birds are presented first. Few species can be considered purely as salt marsh inhabitants. Many of the birds discussed here are frequently seen on tidal flats, tidal pools, and creeks or in the bays and estuaries associated with salt marshes. Next, a few reptiles are described—again, those that are not necessarily at home in the marsh but that visit there from time to time. Mammals are treated like the reptiles; only a few are described, those most likely to be seen.

Fish are not presented as individual species in this book, as they are difficult to collect and even more difficult to identify, the young often being totally unlike the adult in color and general appearance.

Red-throated loon

Gavia stellata

SIZE: 24 to 27 inches

Not commonly seen, this loon winters on the temperate Atlantic coast. It can be distinguished from the common loon (*Gavia immer*) by its slightly upturned bill and a lighter appearance due to its spotted back. The red throat is seen only during the mating season, when the bird is in the Arctic.

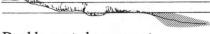

Double-crested cormorant

Phalacrocorax auritus

SIZE: 30 to 35 inches

Though not a true inhabitant of the salt marsh, this cormorant is so common in the northern half of our range that it may be seen fishing nearly anywhere there is food. It dives out of sight, emerges with a fish seemingly too large to eat, and swallows it with surprising ease. Characteristic of cormorants is their need to dry out by spreading their wings after a fishing trip.

Great blue heron

Ardea herodias

SIZE: 48 inches

In the summer this tall, shiny blue-gray heron is seen standing motionlessly in shallow marsh water, waiting for any unwary fish to swim within range of its sharp-pointed, lightning-fast bill. It is easily identified by its size, being the largest wading bird on the Atlantic coast. In the winter it is rarely seen north of southern New England.

Little blue heron

Florida caerulea

SIZE: 20 to 30 inches

DARK BILL

DARK LEGS

This is a small heron that is snowy-white as a youngster, dark gray-blue when an adult. A blue-gray heron patched with white is unmistakably an immature little blue heron approaching adulthood.

Common egret, American egret

Casmerodius albus

SIZE: 37 to 40 inches

YELLOW BILL

DARK LEGS

This is the largest white heron in our range. Like the great blue, it remains motionless when seeking food, awaiting prey to swim within range.

75

Snowy egret

Leucophoyx thula

SIZE: 20 to 30 inches (average 24 inches)

The snowy egret is a medium-sized white heron with black legs and yellow feet. It dashes about the salt marsh, and its voice is limited to a hiss.

Louisiana heron, tricolored heron

Hydranassa tricolor

SIZE: 24 to 28 inches

This is one of the most abundant herons on the Atlantic coast. Its attractive colors and graceful flight make it a rewarding sight.

Yellow-crowned night heron

Nyctanassa violacea

SIZE: 24 inches

Usually a southern dweller, the yellow-crowned heron is a shy bird, flying off with a raspy squawk when disturbed and not returning until the danger has passed. It feeds day and night on crabs and insects.

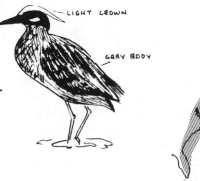

Black-crowned night heron

Nycticorax nycticorax

SIZE: 25 inches

The black-crowned heron is a squat, short-legged, night-feeding bird of the salt marsh. When disturbed in its crowded rookery it takes to the air, emitting loud squawks.

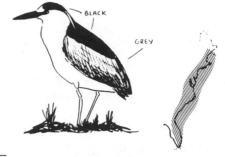

American bittern

Botaurus lentiginosus

SIZE: 24 inches

The American bittern is best known for its camouflage techniques. When approached it stands upright, absolutely still, with its bill pointed straight upward, blending with the surrounding tall grass. Its call is an "oong-kachoonk." When alarmed it emits a croaking sound, "kaw-kaw-kaw."

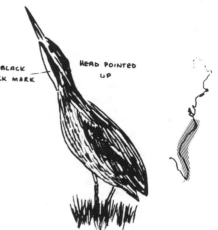

Glossy ibis

Plegadis falcinellus

SIZE: 22 inches

This is the only dark, shiny ibis with a downward-turned bill likely to be seen in our range. Its voice is a simple grunt or bleat.

Mute swan

Cygnus olor

SIZE: 60 inches

The royal bird of England, this graceful animal was introduced into North America and now is established on the central Atlantic coast.

Whistling swan

Olor columbianus

SIZE: 52 inches

Its black, knobless bill distinguishes the whistling from the mute swan. The mute does no better than hiss, while the whistler whoops and trumpets softly.

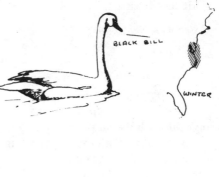

Canada goose

Branta canadensis

SIZE: Up to 43 inches

The Canada goose is so widespread in North America that it could well have been named the North American goose. A vee of these geese heading south is a sure sign of approaching winter. Not all of them migrate, however, and they may be seen year round in many areas of the Atlantic coast.

Brant

Branta bernicla

SIZE: 24 inches

This small goose confines itself to coastal waters. It can be recognized by its black breast.

Snow goose, greater snow goose

Chen hyperborea atlantica

SIZE: 23 to 40 inches

In the winter, snow geese congregate on the central Atlantic coast and feed on the marsh grasses. They are distinguished by white plumage with black wing tips.

Mallard

Anas platyrhynchos

SIZE: 23 inches

Mallards do not restrict their habitat and may be found in nearly any body of water. The green head and white neck band of the male make him easy to identify. The female is similar to many other ducks; look for an orange bill, a whitish tail, and white borders on the blue wing bars.

79

Black duck

Anas rubripes

SIZE: 23 inches

Male and female black ducks are hard to distinguish from one another. They frequent the same habitats as the mallard. In the winter the black duck feeds on blue mussels, periwinkles, and limpets.

Gadwall

Anas strepera

SIZE: 20 inches

The gadwall is rarely seen north of Delaware. Its white wing bar will distinguish it from most other ducks.

Pintail

Anas acuta

SIZE: 22 to 27 inches

As the name implies, a long, pointed tail identifies this male duck. It feeds in the coastal areas during the winter.

Green-winged teal

Anas carolinensis

SIZE: 14 inches

Broad, deep green wing bars with light borders distinguish this small duck from other teal. The male has a green head patch; the female is brownish-gray all over.

Canvasback

Aythya valisneria

SIZE: 21 inches

A canvasback is distinguished by its red head and sloping bill, which merges with the forehead. Groups fly in vees, much like Canada geese.

Bufflehead

Bucephala albeola

SIZE: 14 inches

This is a small, chunky bird with a proportionally large and puffy head. It is basically a sharply contrasting black-and-white. It flies with rapid wingbeats close to the water.

Black rail

Laterallus jamaicensis

SIZE: 6 inches

The sparrow-sized rail is rarely seen. It runs about in the short grasses and sedges of the salt marsh, hardly ever taking flight. One fortunate enough to get a glimpse of it can recognize it by the white spots on its especially dark body.

Semipalmated plover

Charadrius semipalmatus

SIZE: 7 inches

This plover gathers in flocks on the tidal flats for shellfish, sea worms, and other such delicacies. Its sharply defined black-and-white collar, black-and-white forehead, and short bill set it apart from other plovers.

Piping plover

Charadrius melodus

SIZE: 7 inches

The piping plover's call, a bell-like "peep-lo," gives it its nickname of "peep." Its coloration, sandy gray-brown, makes it seem to disappear on the beach when it stops and crouches.

Wilson's plover

Charadrius wilsonia

SIZE: 8 inches

Of the plovers in our range, Wilson's has the largest bill. It feeds on a variety of invertebrates on the tidal flats.

Black-bellied plover

Squatarola squatarola

SIZE: 10 to 13 inches

This, the largest plover in our range, is easily distinguished by its black breast and speckled back.

Ruddy turnstone

Arenaria interpres

SIZE: 9 inches

The ruddy turnstone is known by many names, including "calico turnstone" because of the rust-red marking on its back—a sure way to identify it. A nesting turnstone will even attack a man to defend its eggs.

Common snipe

Capella gallinago

SIZE: 11 inches

A long bill and white stripes on the side of the head identify the common snipe. Active in early morning and at dusk, it is rarely seen during daytime.

Willet

Catoptrophorus semipalmatus

SIZE: 15 inches

In the spring the willet sings a variety of songs in the salt marshes. In flight, its only distinctive marking, a broad white stripe on each black-tipped wing, can be seen.

Greater yellowleg

Totanus melanoleucus

SIZE: 14 inches

An early spring migrant, the greater yellowleg visits the coastal marshes and creeks on its way to its far northern breeding grounds. As the name implies, the long, yellow, stiltlike legs are its best field mark. Its song is a "whew-whew-whew." It prefers fish for food but will accept insects and crustaceans.

YELLOW LEGS

Lesser yellowleg

Totanus flavipes

SIZE: 11 inches

Somewhat smaller in size, the lesser
yellowleg is otherwise quite similar to
the greater. It shares the same habitats
but is a later migrator, not arriving in
our area until late spring on its way
north. You are more likely to see
these birds in the fall or late summer,
as more of them use the Atlantic
coast flyway on their way south.

Least sandpiper

Erolia minutilla

SIZE: 6 inches

This is the smallest shore bird in our
range. Yellow legs and a white line
over the eyes help to identify it. It takes
a variety of foods on the mud flats.

— YELLOW — GREEN LEGS

Semipalmated sandpiper

Ereunetes pusillus

SIZE: 6¼ inches

This is another common peep that
visits our coast during migration,
differing from most others in its black
legs. It follows the receding waves,
probing for insects and crustaceans.

— BLACK LEGS

Marbled godwit

Limosa fedoa

SIZE: 16 to 20 inches

Named for its call, "god-wit," this is
one of our largest shore birds. Having
been overhunted, however, it is a rare
sight in our marshes. A slightly
turned-up bill, marbled back, and
large size identify it.

Sanderling

Crocethia alba

SIZE: 8 inches

In the winter this small, light-colored
bird is the real wave chaser, following
each wave in and out, picking up any
small animals left stranded. Its
migratory route ranks among the
longest—from the Arctic to South
America and back every year.

Black skimmer

Rhynchops nigra

SIZE: 18 inches

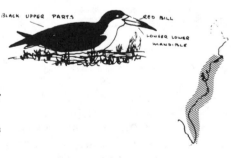

One of the most interesting sights in
bays and estuaries is a black skimmer
flying just above the water, its long
lower mandible skimming the surface
for small fish and other small
organisms.

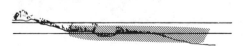

Fish crow

Corvus ossifragus

SIZE: 17 inches

The fish crow is slightly smaller than, but otherwise nearly identical to, the common crow. It favors dead fish in its diet but will accept a large variety of both plant and animal material.

King eider

Somateria spectabilis

SIZE: 22 inches

There is no mistaking a king eider. The large orange shield on its forehead and the distinctly black-and-white body easily identify it.

Common eider

Somateria mollissima

SIZE: 24 inches

A thick, triangular bill forming a straight line to the top of the head, a broad back, and black sides are the field marks of the common eider.

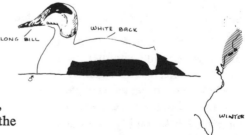

Common scoter

Oidemia nigra

SIZE: 19 inches

The male common scoter is the only wholly black duck with a yellow-orange knob at the base of the bill. The female is brown, with a black crown and white cheek patches. These ducks show a marked preference for shellfish.

Red-breasted merganser

Mergus serrator

SIZE: 22 inches

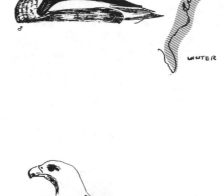

Both male and female have a distinct double crest. The male's head is metallic green, the female's rust-brown. Its diet includes fish, crustaceans, and other shellfish.

Bald eagle

Haliaeetus leucocephalus

SIZE: Up to 36 inches; wingspan to 7 feet

A bird with a seven-foot wingspan and a white head can only be our familiar bald eagle. In coastal areas the bald eagle has a habit of stealing fish from ospreys. As with other birds of prey, it is becoming a rare sight, succumbing to the effects of pesticides.

Osprey, fish eagle, fish hawk

Pandion haliaetus

SIZE: Up to 24 inches; wingspan to 6 feet

This is the only hawk in our range that
dives into the water for its food. In
flight, it is distinguished by the sharp
bend in its wings. Nests, near the
water, are high up in trees. The osprey
population has sharply declined
because of its vulnerability to
pesticides, which reduce the
calcium content of the
eggshells, making them
soft and easily broken.

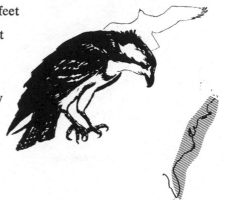

Sparrow hawk, kestrel

Falco sparverius

SIZE: Up to 11 inches

The male sparrow hawk has rust-red
markings on its back and tail,
blue-gray wings, and the black mask
over its eyes that is typical of falcons.
At a distance, the sparrow hawk can
be identified by its habit of hovering
with fast wingbeats and by its sharp
call, "killy-killy-killy."

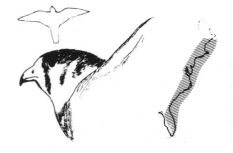

Marsh hawk

Circus cyaneus

SIZE: Up to 22 inches

RING AROUND FACE

Look for narrow wings, a slim tail, and a whitish underside to identify this hawk. A close view shows a distinctive white ring around the face. Its food consists of small birds and mammals.

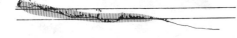

Great black-backed gull

Larus marinus

SIZE: 24 inches; wingspan over 4½ feet

White head and slate-colored back identify the great black-backed gull. It is distinguished from the herring gull by its larger size, whiter breast, and darker back.

Herring gull

Larus argentatus

SIZE: 24 inches; wingspan over 4½ feet

This is our largest gray-mantled gull. It is also the most frequently seen, and has the widest range of all gulls on the Atlantic coast.

Ring-billed gull

Larus delawarensis

SIZE: 19 inches

The ring-billed gull looks like a small herring gull except for the black ring on its bill.

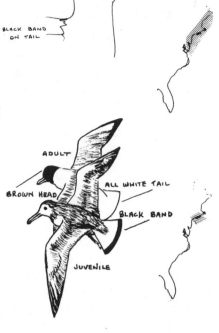

Black-headed gull

Larus ridibundus

SIZE: 15 inches

This is a European gull that visits our coast regularly. Its brown head easily distinguishes it from our native species.

Bonaparte's gull

Larus philadelphia

SIZE: 13 inches

Bonaparte's gull is a small bird in comparison with most of our gulls. Its black head and small size make it easy to identify. In the summer it breeds in the northwestern United States; we see it on the southern Atlantic coast in the late fall and winter. On occasion it comes as far north as Massachusetts.

Laughing gull

Larus atricilla

SIZE: 17 inches; wingspan 3 feet

The solid-black head and dark gray mantle along with the characteristic "laughing" call of this gull are familiar throughout most of the Atlantic coast.

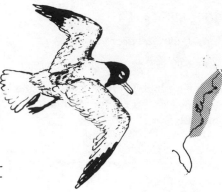

Gull-billed tern

Gelochelidon nilotica

SIZE: 14 inches

This tern will eat almost anything. It will eat insects when fish are not available, and even resort to other small animals in the salt marsh when both fish and insects are not sufficient for its appetite. It is identified by a large black, gull-like bill and black-capped head.

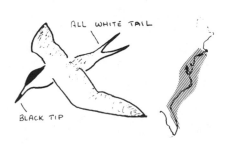

LARGE BLACK BILL

BLACK FEET

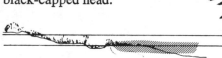

Forster's tern

Sterna forsteri

SIZE: 15 inches

Only slightly larger than the gull-billed tern, Forster's tern has a yellow-orange bill tipped with black. It is similar to the common tern except that it lacks the latter's dark tail tips.

ALL WHITE TAIL

BLACK TIP

Common tern

Sterna hirundo

SIZE: 15 inches

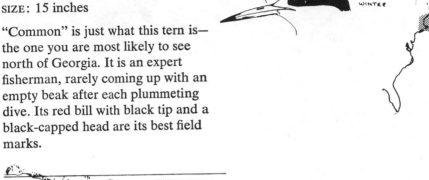

"Common" is just what this tern is—the one you are most likely to see north of Georgia. It is an expert fisherman, rarely coming up with an empty beak after each plummeting dive. Its red bill with black tip and a black-capped head are its best field marks.

Roseate tern

Sterna dougallii

SIZE: 14 to 17 inches

A slightly pink tinge to its plumage during breeding season gives the roseate tern its name. It has a longer tail than the common tern, and its bill, usually black, may show some red.

Least tern

Sterna albifrons

SIZE: 9 inches

The least tern is the smallest tern on the Atlantic coast, and the only one with a yellow bill.

Seaside sparrow

Ammospiza maritima

SIZE: 5 to 6 inches

This sparrow is not generally thought of as a salt marsh inhabitant, probably because it is so secretive. Its rather plain song, "cut-cut-chee," is usually the only sign of its presence in the marsh. It is a dark olive-gray, with a yellow streak just in front of the eyes and a white line along the jaw.

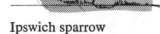

Ipswich sparrow

Passerculus princeps

SIZE: 6 inches

At the edge of the marsh and in the dune grasses, the Ipswich sparrow can be seen jumping about erratically or flitting nervously close to the ground. It is a sand-colored bird that can be identified by its two light wing bars and a white streak on the crown. In the spring there is a distinct yellow stripe in front of the eyes. If you fail to see this bird, you may well hear his song, "tsi-tsi-tsit-tsee-tsayy."

Snow bunting

Plectrophenax nivalis

SIZE: 7 inches

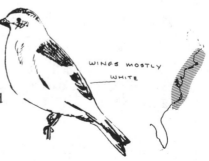

The snow bunting breeds in the far north, visiting our area in the fall and winter, and is the whitest-appearing land bird we see.

Mud turtle

Kinosternon subrubrum

SIZE: Up to 3½ inches

The mud turtle may be found hunting for insects near the high-tide line. Look for yellow spots on the sides of the head and a smooth carapace to identify it.

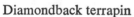

Diamondback terrapin

Malaclemys terrapin

SIZE: Up to 8 inches

This turtle wanders well into the intertidal zone looking for a variety of food, both vegetable and animal. Its head and forelegs have white spots, and it has white lips. The carapace is rough and divided into distinct squares.

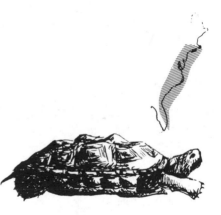

Painted turtle

Chrysemys picta

SIZE: Up to 9 inches

In quiet brackish waters, the painted turtle forages about for plants, insects, mollusks, and other foods. The red streaks on the sides of the head and the brilliant red markings under the edge of the carapace unmistakably distinguish it from other turtles.

Loggerhead turtle

Caretta caretta

SIZE: Up to 3 feet

Loggerheads are strictly marine, as
evidenced by their having flippers
instead of feet. Each front flipper has
two small claws, and there are five
(occasionally four) large plates on
each side of the carapace.

Cottonmouth, water moccasin

Agkistrodon piscivorus

SIZE: Up to 6 feet

In the southernmost reaches of our
range, the poisonous cottonmouth
stalks turtles, fish, or rodents that
wander too close to the water. The
adult snake appears black; juveniles
show black bands on a dark brown
background. The large diamond-
shaped head identifies it as a pit viper
and should be adequate warning to
the observer to stay away.

Brown water snake

Natrix taxispilota

SIZE: Up to 6 feet

It is unlikely that you will encounter a
snake in the salt marsh. If you do, it
will probably be a brown water
snake—distinguished by small, bulging
eyes, a long, narrow head, and black-
bordered dark spots on a heavy body
whose color may vary from red-brown
to green-brown.

MAMMALS—Class *Mammalia*

Gray squirrel

Sciurus carolinensis

SIZE: Body, up to 10 inches;
tail, up to 10 inches

The gray squirrel seems to be every-
where. Whether it is or not, its tracks
are often seen in the mud and sand of
the tidal flats. The seeds of the various
salt marsh grasses readily attract it.

Deer mouse

Peromyscus maniculatus

SIZE: Head and body, up to 5 inches; tail, up to 5 inches

The deer mouse, being primarily
nocturnal, is rarely seen, but its
presence on the upper intertidal flats
and the dunes is evidenced by its
tracks.

Meadow vole

Microtus pennsylvanicus

SIZE: Body, up to 5 inches; tail, up to 2½ inches

The signs of the meadow vole are grass cut off at the stems and brown droppings. It may also be possible to catch a glimpse of it in the daytime. Its tracks may well cross a tidal creek, as it is a good swimmer.

Muskrat

Ondatra zibethicus

SIZE: Body, up to 14 inches; tail, up to 11 inches

The muskrat's presence in the salt marsh is unmistakable because of its conspicuous cone-shaped lodges. It is the most aquatic of salt marsh mammals and has established large colonies in some coastal marshes.

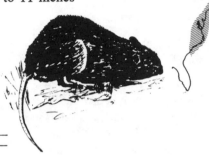

Norway rat

Rattus norvegicus

SIZE: Body, up to 10 inches; tail, up to 8 inches

Even the most avid conservationist finds it hard to get enthusiastic over the presence of a Norway rat. It is nevertheless commonly seen in the salt marsh, eating carrion and attacking young birds in the nesting season.

Black rat

Rattus rattus

SIZE: Body, up to 7 inches; tail, up to 9 inches

The black rat differs from the Norway
rat in having a tail longer than its body.
Its color may be black or brown, and
it is less common in the marshes than
the Norway rat.

White-tailed deer, Virginia deer

Odocoileus virginianus

SIZE: Up to more than 3½ feet wide
across shoulders; 6 feet long
(adult average)

This is the largest mammal likely to be
seen in the salt marsh. It often grazes
on salt meadow grasses.

NATIONAL WILDLIFE REFUGES

The following is a list of National Wildlife Refuges, by location, where the species described in the book can be found. Descriptive pamphlets are available by writing to: United States Department of the Interior, Fish and Wildlife Service, Bureau of Sports Fisheries and Wildlife, Washington, D.C. 20240.

MAINE
Moosehorn—Calais
Rachel Carson—Wells

MASSACHUSETTS
Parker River—Newburyport
Monomoy—Chatham

NEW YORK
Morton—Sag Harbor
Target Rock—Huntington

NEW JERSEY
Barnegat—Manahawkin
Brigantine—Oceanville

DELAWARE
Prime Hook—Milford

MARYLAND
Eastern Neck—Rock Hill
Blackwater—Cambridge

VIRGINIA
Chincoteague—Chincoteague
Fisherman Island—Northampton County
Back Bay—Virginia Beach
Mackay Island—Virginia Beach

NORTH CAROLINA
Pea Island—Manteo
Mattamuskeet—New Holland
Cedar Island—Cedar Island

SOUTH CAROLINA
Cape Romain—Awendaw

GEORGIA
Tybee—Chatham County
Wassaw—Chatham County
Blackbeard—McIntosh County
Wolf Island—McIntosh County

The wildlife refuges listed here are federally managed. There are numerous other refuges or sanctuaries locally maintained which are definitely worth visiting. Your local government will provide you with information regarding these areas.

GLOSSARY OF TERMS

Alga   A simple photosynthetic plant, most species of which are aquatic. Marine varieties are commonly called seaweed.

Carapace   The hard upper covering (shell) of turtles and crustaceans.

Carnivore   An animal which feeds primarily on the flesh of other animals.

Crustacean   A chiefly aquatic arthropod with a hard outer covering, or exoskeleton.

Detritus   Disintegrated matter—mineral, plant, or animal.

Diatom   A minute unicellular alga of Class *Bacillariophyceae,* composed of two overlapping parts containing silica.

Ecosystem   A total community of mineral, vegetable, and animal interaction.

Ecotone   An environment where two different ecosystems merge.

Estuary   A protected body of water in which the sea and a river meet.

Field Mark   A conspicuous marking used as a point of identification.

Fucoid   An alga belonging to Order FUCALES, including brown algae such as Genus *Fucus.*

Herbivore   A species subsisting primarily on plants.

Holdfast   A base part of the stem of some algae which anchors the plant to a hard substratum.

Hydroid   An invertebrate of Class *Hydrozoa* that is colonial and forms asexual polyps.

Intertidal Zone   The area between the high- and low-tide limits.

Invertebrate   An animal lacking a backbone or spinal cord.

Kelp   Any of many brown algae, usually referring to the larger varieties.

Larva   An early (juvenile) development stage of an animal which differs from the adult form.

Littoral Zone   A shallow aquatic environment, such as coastal water and the intertidal zone.

Mandible   A jaw, upper or lower, as of a bird's beak.

Medusa   The sexual, free-swimming form of **Phylum COELENTERATA**, usually bell-shaped.

Metazoan   An animal of more than one cell.

Mollusk   A bilaterally symmetrical shellfish of **Phylum MOLLUSCA**.

Neap Tide   Tide of minimum distance between the high and low marks.

Nocturnal   Active primarily at night.

Pelagic   Associated with, pertaining to, or dependent upon the open ocean.

Phylum   A major division of living organisms between kingdom and class.

Phytoplankton   Minute floating aquatic plants.

Planktont   A free-floating or weakly swimming aquatic organism.

Polyp   A hollow cylindrical body closed and attached at one end, open at the other (the mouth).

Predator   An animal that subsists on other animals.

Protozoan   A unicellular animal of **Phylum PROTOZOA**.

Rockweed   A brown coastal alga of Genus *Fucus* or *Ascophyllum*.

Salt Pan   A poorly drained tidal area where sea salt is concentrated by evaporation.

Sargassum   The common name of a group of planktonic brown seaweeds.

Spermatophyte   A plant that produces seeds.

Spikelet   A small cluster of grass flowers.

Spring Tide   Tide of maximum distance between the high and low marks.

Substratum   A surface to which an organism is attached.

Temperate   Referring to the moderate (middle) climatic zone, between the Tropic and Arctic zones.

Tentacle   A hairlike unsegmented protrusion of an organism.

Tidal Creek   A riverlike body of water in the intertidal zone whose depth varies with the tides.

Tidal Pool   A pool of marine water in the intertidal zone which varies in depth with the tides.

Tidemarsh   A marine wetland owing its characteristics to the tides.

Vertebrate   An animal with a backbone.

BIBLIOGRAPHY

Dales, R. P., *Practical Invertebrate Zoology*. University of Washington Press, Seattle, 1970.

Wetmore, A., *Water, Prey & Game Birds of North America*. National Geographic Society, Washington, D.C., 1965.

Newell, G. E., and R. C. Newell, *Marine Plankton: A Practical Guide*. Hutchinson Educational Ltd., London, 1963.

Nichols, D., J. Cooke, and D. Whiteley, *The Oxford Book of Invertebrates*. Oxford University Press, England, 1971.

Miller, R. C., *The Sea*. Random House, New York, 1966.

Amos, W. H., *The Life of the Seashore*, Our Living World of Nature. McGraw-Hill, New York, 1966.

Martin, A. C., H. S. Zim, and A. L. Nelson, *American Wildlife & Plants: A Guide to Wildlife Food Habits*. Dover, New York, 1951.

MacGinitie, G. E., and N. MacGinitie, *Natural History of Marine Animals*. McGraw-Hill, New York, 1949.

Wimpenny, R. S., *The Plankton of the Sea*. American Elsevier, New York, 1966.

Petry, L. C., and M. G. Norman, *A Beachcomber's Botany*. The Chatham Conservation Foundation Inc., Chatham, Mass., 1968.

Robinson, B. L., and M. L. Fernald, *Gray's New Manual of Botany: A Handbook of the Flowering Plants and Ferns* (seventh ed.). American Book Co., London, 1908.

Kingsbury, J. M., *Seaweeds of Cape Cod and the Islands*. Chatham Press, Chatham, Mass., 1969.

Giambarba, P., *What Is It? at the Beach*. Scrimshaw Press, Barre, Mass., 1969.

Knobel, E., *The Grasses, Sedges & Rushes of the Northern United States*. Bradlee Whidden, Boston, 1899.

Green, J., *The Biology of Estuarine Animals*. University of Washington, Seattle, 1968.

Webber, E. E., and R. T. Wilce, "Benthic Salt Marsh Algae at Ipswich, Massachusetts," *Rhodora*. Vol. 73, pp. 262–291, 1971.

Webber, E. E., "Seasonal Occurrence and Ecology of Salt Marsh Phanerogams at Ipswich, Massachusetts," *Rhodora*. Vol. 70, pp. 442–450, 1968.

Webber, E. E., "Observations on Microcoleus Lyngbaceus (Kutz) Crouan from Marine Habitata in New England," *Rhodora*. Vol. 73, pp. 238–243, 1971.

Ramus, J., "Codium: The Invader," *Discovery*. Pp. 59–68, Spring 1971.

Wilce, R. T., "A Revision of the North Atlantic Species of the Simplices Section of Laminaria," *Studies in the Genus Laminaria* (reprint *Botanica Gothoburgensia* III, Proceedings of the Fifth Marine Biological Symposium, Goteborg). University of Massachusetts, Amherst, 1965.

Taylor, W. R., *Marine Algae of the Northeastern Coast of North America*. University of Michigan, Ann Arbor, 1957.

Peterson, R. T., *A Field Guide to the Birds*. Houghton Mifflin, Boston, 1947.

Zim, H. S., and I. N. Gabrielson, *Birds: A Guide to the Most Familiar American Birds*. Golden Press, New York, 1949.

Sprunt, A., IV, and H. S. Zim, *Gamebirds*. Golden Press, New York, 1961.

Hanley, W., *Nature's Ways*. Massachusetts Audubon Society, Lincoln, 1971.

Hay, J., and P. Farb, *The Atlantic Shore*. Harper & Row, New York, 1966.

Hitchcock, A. S., *Manual of the Grasses of the U.S.* U.S. Department of Agriculture, Washington, D.C., 1950.

Marshall, N., and O. Marshall, *Ocean Life*. Macmillan, New York, 1971.

Shackleton, K., and T. Stokes, *Birds of the Atlantic Ocean*. Country Life, Middlesex, England, 1968.

INDEX

105

bufflehead, 81
Bugula turrita, 51

Calanus finmarchicus, 10
calico crab, 61
Callinectes sapidus, 61
Callithamnion corymbosum, 28
Callothrix sp., 15
Canada goose, 78
Cancer irroratus, 62
Cancer sp., 11
canvasback, 81
Capella gallinago, 84
Carcinus maenas, 60
Carcinus sp., 11
Caretta caretta, 96
Carolina marsh clam, 69
Caryophyllaceae, 35
Casmerodius albus, 75
Catoptrophorus semipalmatus, 84
cattails, 40
Ceramium rubrum, 27
Cerebratulus lacteus, 49
Ceriantheopsis americanus, 48
CHAETOGNATHA, 50
Chaetomorpha melagonium, 18
Chaetorceros sp., 7
chairmaker's rush, 41
Charadrius melodus, 82
Charadrius semipalmatus, 82
Charadrius wilsonia, 83
Chen hyperborea atlantica, 79
Chenopodiaceae, 33–35
Chenopodium rubrum, 35
chicken claws, 34
china-back fiddler crab, 61
CHLOROPHYTA, 16–19
Chondrus crispus, 24
Chrysemys picta, 95
Chrysophyceae, 23
CHRYSOPHYTA, 6–7, 14, 23
Circus cyaneus, 90
Cladophora gracilis, 18
coast blite, 35
Codium fragile, 19
COELENTERATA, 45–48
coelenterates, 45–48
coiled worm, 55
comb jellies, 48–49
common basket clam, 71
common boat shell, 65
common egret, 75
common eider, 87
common grass shrimp, 59
common ladies' tresses, 38
common moon shell, 66

common moss animal, 50
common periwinkle, 64
common sand flea, 57
common scoter, 88
common snipe, 84
common soft-shell clam, 71
common spider crab, 60
common tern, 93
Compositae, 36–37
composites, 36
consumption weed, 37
Copepoda, 10
copepods, 10
Corbula contracta, 71
Corvus ossifragus, 87
cottonmouth, 96
Crangon septemspinosa, 58
Crassostrea virginica, 70
Crepidula fornicata, 65
Crisia denticulata, 50
Crisia eburnea, 50
Crocethia alba, 86
crustacean plankton, 10
CTENOPHORAE, 48–49
Cucumaria pulcherrima, 53
cup hydroid, 46
Cyanea capillata, 47
CYANOPHYTA, 14–15
Cygnus olor, 78
Cyperaceae, 41–42
Cyperus polystachyos var. texensis, 41
cypris larva, 10
Cystoclonium purpureum, 27

dead man's fingers, 45
deer mouse, 97
Diadumene leucolena, 47
diamondback terrapin, 95
diatoms, 6–7, 23
dinoflagellates, 7
Diodora cayenensis, 63
Diopatra cuprea, 54
Distichlis spicata, 30
double-branching hydroid, 46
double-crested cormorant, 74
dulse, 24

early seaside plantain, 39
ECHINODERMATA, 52–53
echinoderms, 52–53
edible shrimp, 58
eelgrass, 39
Elymus virginicus, 31
Enteromorpha erecta, 17
Enteromorpha intestinalis, 16
Enteromorpha linza, 17

piping plover, 82
plankton, 5–11
Plantaginaceae, 39–40
Plantago juncoides var. decipiens, 39
Plantago oliganthos, 40
plantains, 39–40
plants, 12–42
Plectrophenax nivalis, 94
Plegadis falcinellus, 77
Pleurobrachia pileus, 49
Pleurosigma aestuarii, 7
Pluchea purpurascens var. succulenta, 37
Plumbaginaceae, 42
plumed worm, 54
Polinices duplicatus, 65
Polygonaceae, 32
Polygonum glaucum, 32
Polymesoda caroliniana, 69
Polysiphonia lanosa, 28
pondweeds, 39
PORIFERA, 44–45
Porphyra umbilicalis, 26
Potamogetonaceae, 39
Potentilla anserina, 38
Prasinocladus lubricus, 16
primroses, 36
Primulaceae, 36
PROTOZOA, 7, 8–9
protozoans, 7, 8–9
purple sea urchin, 52

radiolarians, 8
Rattus norvegicus, 98
Rattus rattus, 99
red algae, 24–28
red-breasted merganser, 88
red rock crab, 62
red sponge, 45
red-throated loon, 74
reed, 30
reptiles, 95–97
Reptilia, 95–97
Rhizoclonium riparum, 19
Rhizoclonium sp., 18–19
Rhodochorton purpureum, 25
RHODOPHYTA, 14, 24–28
Rhodymenia palmata, 24
Rhynchops nigra, 86
Rhynchospora macrostachya, 42
ribbed mussel, 68
ribbonworms, 49
ring-billed gull, 91
Rivularia atra, 15
rock barnacle, 56
rock crab, 62
rock purple, 66

rockweed, 19, 20, 21
Rosaceae, 38
roseate tern, 93
roses, 38
rough periwinkle, 64
ruddy turnstone, 83
rushes, 32–33

Sagitta hexaptera, 50
Salicornia bigelovii, 34
Salicornia europaea, 34
Salicornia virginica, 34
salt hay, 29
salt marsh bulrush, 41
salt marsh cordgrass, 29
salt marsh fleabane, 37
salt marsh periwinkle, 65
salt meadow grass, 29
salt reed grass, 29
samphire, 34
sanderling, 86
sand shrimp, 58
sand spurry, 35
sargassum, 21
Sargassum filipendula, 21
Scirpus americanus, 41
Scirpus maritimus, 41
Sciurus carolinensis, 97
Scomber scombrus, 11
screw auger, 38
Scrophulariaceae, 39
Scypha lingua, 44
seabeach amaranth, 38
seabeach knotgrass, 32
seabeach knotweed, 32
seabeach orach, 33
sea blite, 35
sea gooseberry, 49
sea lavender, 42
sea lettuce, 17
sea mat, 51
sea milkwort, 36
sea mouse, 53
sea myrtle, 37
seaside gerardia, 39
seaside goldenrod, 36
seaside sparrow, 94
seaside wild rye, 31
sea walnut, 49
seaweed hopper, 57
seaweeds, 13, 14–28
sedges, 41–42
segmented worms, 53–55
Seirospora griffithsiana, 28
semipalmated plover, 82

semipalmated sandpiper, 85
shark eye, 65
silverweed, 38
silvery hydroid, 46
Sisyrinchium arenicola, 42
skeleton shrimp, 58
slender-leaved aster, 36
slipper comb jelly, 49
smaller clam worm, 54
smooth cordgrass, 29
smooth periwinkle, 64
smooth-scaled worm, 54
snail fur, 45
snow bunting, 94
snow goose, 79
snowy egret, 76
soft rush, 32
soft-shell crab, 61
Solidago sempervirens, 36
Somateria mollissima, 87
Somateria spectabilis, 87
sparrow hawk, 89
Spartina alterniflora, 13, 29
Spartina cynosuroides, 29
Spartina patens, 13, 29
Spartina pectinata, 30
Spergularia marina, 35
spike grass, 30
Spiranthes cernua, 38
Spirorbis borealis, 55
sponges, 44–45
Squatarola squatarola, 83
Squilla empusa, 59
star coral, 48
steamer clam, 71
Sterna albifrons, 93
Sterna dougallii, 93
Sterna forsteri, 92
Sterna hirundo, 93
stinkweed, 37
stout razor, 70
Strongylocentrotus droehbachiensis, 52
Suaeda maritima, 35
sugar kelp, 22
sun jellyfish, 47
switch grass, 32

Tagelus plebeius, 70
Talorchestia longicornis, 57
Terrell grass, 31
Thais lapillus, 66
Thuiaria argentea, 46
tortoise-shell limpet, 63
Totanus flavipes, 85
Totanus melanoleucus, 84
tricolored heron, 76
tufted sponge, 44
turreted moss animal, 51
Typha angustifolia, 40
Typhaceae, 40
Typha latifolia, 40
typical orach, 33

Uca pugilator, 61
Uca pugnax, 60
Ulothrix flacca, 16
Ulva lactuca, 17
Urosalpinx cinerea, 66

Vaucheria sp., 23
vertebrates, 72–99
Virginia deer, 99
Virginia oyster, 70

water moccasin, 96
whistling swan, 78
white-tailed deer, 99
willet, 84
Wilson's plover, 83
woody glasswort, 34
wormlike sea cucumber, 53
worm sea anemone, 48
wrack, 21

Xanthophyceae, 23

yellow-crowned night heron, 76
yellow-green algae, 23

zoea larva, 11
zonation, 13
zooplankton, 8–11
Zostera marina, 13, 39